Global Consequences of Russia's Invasion of Ukraine

Grzegorz W. Kolodko

Global Consequences of Russia's Invasion of Ukraine

The Economics and Politics of the Second Cold War

Grzegorz W. Kolodko 🆔
Transformation, Integration
and Globalization Economic Research
(TIGER)
Kozminski University
Warsaw, Poland

ISBN 978-3-031-24262-5   ISBN 978-3-031-24263-2   (eBook)
https://doi.org/10.1007/978-3-031-24263-2

© The Editor(s) (if applicable) and The Author(s), under exclusive license to Springer Nature Switzerland AG 2023
This work is subject to copyright. All rights are solely and exclusively licensed by the Publisher, whether the whole or part of the material is concerned, specifically the rights of translation, reprinting, reuse of illustrations, recitation, broadcasting, reproduction on microfilms or in any other physical way, and transmission or information storage and retrieval, electronic adaptation, computer software, or by similar or dissimilar methodology now known or hereafter developed.
The use of general descriptive names, registered names, trademarks, service marks, etc. in this publication does not imply, even in the absence of a specific statement, that such names are exempt from the relevant protective laws and regulations and therefore free for general use.
The publisher, the authors, and the editors are safe to assume that the advice and information in this book are believed to be true and accurate at the date of publication. Neither the publisher nor the authors or the editors give a warranty, expressed or implied, with respect to the material contained herein or for any errors or omissions that may have been made. The publisher remains neutral with regard to jurisdictional claims in published maps and institutional affiliations.

This Springer imprint is published by the registered company Springer Nature Switzerland AG
The registered company address is: Gewerbestrasse 11, 6330 Cham, Switzerland

I have adhered to my rule of never criticizing any measure of war or policy after the event unless I had before expressed publicly or formally my opinion or warning about it.

Winston Churchill (1874–1965)

*To those who fight for peace
without preparing for war*

Contents

1	**In a Dark Shadow**	1
	Notes	3
2	**This World of Ours Got into a Trap**	5
	Notes	9
3	**Nothing Justifies Russia's Invasion of Ukraine**	11
	Notes	16
4	**The US Should not Provoke Taiwan to Declare Independence**	19
	Notes	25
5	**The Fifth Partition of Poland is Being Prepared?**	29
	Notes	34
6	**How Many Years Will This War Last?**	35
	Notes	45
7	**Against Whom the People's Anger Turns**	49
	Notes	52
8	**The Economics of Sanctions Work Differently from Their Politics**	55
	Notes	62
9	**Sanctions Are Intended to Bring About the Results Desired by Their Enforcers**	65
	Notes	70

10	Great Inflation Is a Delayed Invoice for the Pandemic and a Prepayment for the War	73
	Notes	80
11	A Very Expensive War is Getting Even More Expensive	81
	Notes	84
12	Globalization Has Taken a Few Powerful Blows But Has not Been Knocked Out	87
	Notes	91
13	Help Ukraine to Rise from the Ruins	93
	Notes	99
14	The Second Cold War is a World War	101
	Notes	110
15	The More NATO Grows, the Less Secure Europe Is?	113
	Notes	120
16	Nostalgia for Authoritarian Regimes Sets In	123
	Notes	130
17	All Scenarios Are Black, Although the Geography of the Frying Will Vary	133
	Notes	136
18	Where to Get These Billions and Trillions	137
	Notes	144
19	Euro-Atlantic and Euro-Asian Mega-Systems Can Peacefully Compete and Cooperate	145
	Notes	148
20	Something Far Worse Than the Seven Plagues of the Bible	149
	Notes	154
Bibliography		155
Index		159

1

In a Dark Shadow

War!

What war? Peace! Only that in yet another part of the vast world, a local armed conflict has erupted on yet another frontier. It is getting all the publicity because it is in Eastern Europe, close to the rich West, whose interests and ideas are at stake. It is so loud about it, because a global power, this time Russia, got involved in it. In the same way that the Vietnam War was once so much talked about because it was fought by the powerful United States. They lost then and Russia will lose now. When? Even if not soon, time is moving fast. We should therefore keep calm…

Well, it is impossible to keep calm, although the further away from the Donbas and southern Ukraine, the further away from Poland and Eastern Europe, the easier it should be. But it is not, which is due to, unprecedented in history, transnational linkages, cultural, political and economic couplings, interconnections related to the natural environment in which we live and die, and the security of people dealing with the hardships of their daily lives far from the front line.

Indeed, there is much to be worried about, but above all one must try to understand as much as possible what is happening and why. For the web of complex interconnections is incredible, as never before in the history of mankind, because of the nature of both war and peace. The level of economic development, its variation, demographic and climate change, globalization of the economy and culture, the impact of science and technology on the lives of individuals and societies, value systems and ways of thinking—all these co-determine the way things are. And—even more importantly—the way things can, and sometimes must happen in the future, which has never in our life been as difficult to predict as it is today. All the more reason to make an effort to grasp intellectually what is happening and what is at stake for whom. Then we will not only be closer to the truth about what is behind us but we will have more reliable information and interpretations to enable us to behave in the future in a reasonably rational manner in this irrational world in times of war and peace.

* * *

Just a while ago, my multifaceted book entitled "Political Economy of New Pragmatism: Implications of Irreversible Globalization",[1] which deals with the political, social and economic problems besetting our world, has been published, and already so many significant facts and processes have taken place that it requires additional interpretation. The circumstances of the numerous issues of great significance discussed in the book have changed much from those of so recent a time when I was finishing that text in the spring of 2022. That is why additional comments are needed or simply an answer to the question of whether and why I sustain a particular opinion in the face of changing realities. In principle, I do sustain my opinions, but certain aspects appear in a new light—or in a dark shadow we have found ourselves in after February 24, 2022, when Russia made its despicable assault on Ukraine—which requires additional reflection and enriched argumentation. The issues that need to be discussed, the problems that need to be addressed and the threads that need to be commented on, are many. Hence this book.

Its contents revolve around what has already been the axis of theoretical and political reflections in the previous volumes of my trilogy on the world, only that now many new things are happening, and a lot of what is not new is happening differently. Still, though, humanity is facing epochal challenges. Meeting them requires lifestyle changes, while the functioning of the economy, different than before, must be correlated with those changes. All this determines the need to redefine the objective of economic activity. These epochal challenges stem from seven overlapping mega-trends which are symptomatic of contemporary times:

1. Demographic changes, especially the aging of the population and huge variations in fertility rates.
2. Environmental changes, especially the depletion of non-renewable resources and climate warming.
3. The scientific and technological revolution, especially the digitization of the economy and culture, as well as automation.
4. Non-inclusive globalization, especially increasing areas of exclusion and growing inequality.
5. The general crisis of neoliberal capitalism, especially the structural economic imbalances.
6. The crisis of liberal democracy, especially the accompanying polarization of societies.
7. The Second Cold War, especially the West-Russia tensions and the US-China conflict.

Undoubtedly, Russian aggression in Ukraine and its complex geopolitical and economic consequences are further confusing the already enormously complicated reality, increasing the area of uncertainty about the future that awaits us. All the more reason to reflect on what the future holds and why. Especially because some have become so involved in war and peace that here we are, in a reality that is better captured by exactly these two words—war and peace.

Notes

1. Grzegorz W. Kolodko, "Political Economy of New Pragmatism: Implications of Irreversible Globalization", Springer, Cham, 2022.

2

This World of Ours Got into a Trap

History just goes on. Over time, when enough of it has passed, it turns out that the events of the past were not at all as they were described by their contemporaries, that something completely different was going on than many of those living at that time believed, because they believed what others told them, although they themselves understood little of what was happening, or because they let themselves be persuaded of obvious lies told for ideological or material reasons, or both. For example, we can read a fascinating book about the First Crusade, a scholarly account by a historian, from which we can learn what really happened on that occasion at the beginning of the twelfth century and who wanted what in this supposedly holy expedition, fought in the name of defending the only right, obviously, faith.[1] Historians still argue about the great revolutions: the American, French and Bolshevik revolutions, let alone the profound cultural, social, economic and political transformations unfolding before our eyes. We will not have to wait that long for a reliable account of the Ukrainian crisis, but surely history hopefully objective—will interpret it quite differently from the current political and media narrative, as well as the quasi-academic political science tale. Once again, let us remind ourselves that things happen the way they do because a lot is happening at the same time. This is also the case with the Russian–Ukrainian conflict—its causes, course, consequences and far-reaching implications. It is therefore worth realizing what is actually happening.

For the fourth time in the twenty-first century, we are being told that the world as we know it has come to an end, that nothing will be like it was before anymore. Such opinions prevailed not only in the media and political circles but also in numerous social scientific studies. This was the case after the terrorist attack by Islamic fundamentalists on the World Trade Center in New York on September 11, 2001. After the global financial and economic crisis of 2008–2010, the world was supposed to be very different from before. The same was said in the context of the devastating, still-lasting COVID-19 pandemic. This is also the case, even more pronounced, now in the face of Russia's aggression against Ukraine. Undoubtedly, each of these tragedies—with all the differences between them, one of the biggest of which is that the crisis at the turn of the first and second decades of this century was foreseeable, as I myself did—leaves a significant mark on the reality around us and strongly affects the future. Therefore, let me reiterate right away, that this world of ours got into a trap, but it can make its way out. It can, it does not have to. Continuity rather than change will dominate.

The changes that the Ukrainian tragedy entails need a lot of attention. The year 2022—probably the first since time immemorial without the silly season, because neither UFOs appeared, nor even the monster emerged from the depths of Loch Ness—is already clearly written in the pages of history. Unlike other exceptional years—recently 1989 was such, which was written in golden letters in connection with the Polish Round Table, the fall of the Berlin Wall and the end of that Cold War—this one is written in black letters.

John Maynard Keynes, I believe the greatest economist of the twentieth century, is reputed to have said that when the situation changes, he changes his views. Well, the situation has changed and some views need to be reviewed. In many cases, it is not so much that they need to be changed—as long as they were right before, at the time they were formulated—but the phenomena and processes of our interest need to be reinterpreted. They are contextual, thus the interpretation of what is happening and why must also be contextual.

It is not enough to be right; one still has to be right at the right time. It may happen that when we expressed a view or made a certain assertion in the past, we were right then, but we are wrong now because the circumstances on which our judgments and conclusions were based are completely different now. If someone claims in the middle of the day that the sun is shining as it can be seen, he or she cannot be criticized for it in the middle of the night with the claim that it is not true because everyone can see that it is the moon that is shining. Shock disorders—and this is what we are dealing with as a result of the reprehensible Russian attack on Ukraine—cause that in many cases a view that seemed or even was correct *ex ante*, before the shock, is no longer so *ex post*. So, given that quite a few new facts have occurred, it is worth reviewing the interpretation of some of them.

I am taking a huge risk in writing these words. By putting my views on highly contentious issues concerning political and economic phenomena, which often change in ways that are extremely difficult, if not impossible, to predict in advance, under fire from critical readers and a wider public, I run the risk of making mistakes when it comes to sketching out alternative scenarios for future changes. Nevertheless, I take this risk out of a sense of my civic and professional duty. It is clear that when referring to the future in times where chaos often dominates over order, questionable assumptions have to be made. In doing so, I rely on a comprehensible knowledge of the facts and their interpretations in terms of social sciences, as well as specific modeling of the emergence of phenomena and the course of processes in the future.

In the second volume of the trilogy about the world, I attempted to show a future that has since become a thing of the past. It is therefore easy to verify what has worked and what has not. Then, just as now, I treat the future in two categories—inevitable and possible. At present, what is bound to happen is far less than what might happen. After all, in order to be able to sensibly move around the murky grounds of diagnoses, assessments and suggestions for actions, it is necessary to know what is really going on and what is at stake for whom in the ongoing games. That is why I am not heeding the advice to wait and only take a position when it becomes clear what will come out of all this; I am already presenting it now.

The Ukrainian catastrophe—for it is a major, multifaceted catastrophe for that country—is unfolding before our eyes and beside us. Yet again, history goes on. It is natural and fully understandable that we observe what is happening in a country close to us with great concern and interest, but how extreme our views can be. It is astonishing to hear totally mutually exclusive—and, worse still, making any dialogue impossible—opinions from people who are wise, educated and familiar with the world. While an eminent scholar, a member of the Polish Academy of Sciences who also lectures at American universities, says that "the fascist state of Russia must be destroyed", his colleague, a member of the Russian Academy of Sciences who also once lectured at British universities, asks: "Can a serious researcher believe that Ukraine with its suppression of political opposition, closing down of mass media, limitation of cultural rights of ethnical non-Ukrainians (not only Russians), genocide-type policies against the Donbas and Lugansk, support (at least acceptance) of Nazist ideology and practices be a democratic state?".

How can we postulate and expect negotiations and dialogue between politicians and generals when even intellectuals are unable to talk to each other? This makes it all the more necessary to seek the truth, search for meaning, strive for reason and resist lies, hypocrisy and downright stupidity.

What is also astonishing is the verbally fully consistent opinion of the rectors of Russian universities from St. Petersburg to Sakhalin, as many as 287 of whom, the Rector's Corps of the Russian Federation, signed an open letter a week after the start of the "special military operation", or simply the war invasion, in Ukraine, expressing their strong support for President Putin's decision "to finally end the eight-year confrontation between Ukraine and the Donbas, achieve the demilitarization and denazification of Ukraine, and thereby protect itself from growing military threats." As they write, "Now more than ever, we must demonstrate confidence and resilience in the face of economic and information attacks, effectively rally around our President, by our example strengthening the optimistic spirit and faith in the power of reason among young people, instilling hope for an early peace."[2] How can one talk about the power of reason in such a mindless way?! What does military power have to do with the logic of reason? Doesn't it come as a surprise that such content can be expressed by scientists, professors and rectors in a country whose culture has given mankind such memorable figures as Pushkin and Dostoyevsky, as Tchaikovsky and Shostakovich, as Repin and Kandinsky? After all, greatness and vanity need not go hand in hand, even if they are separated by centuries.

When I asked a fellow rector, who did not sign the letter, how such a pathetic act by people of above-average intelligence and knowledge was even possible, he wrote me back: "They really think so (minority) and they are afraid of the consequences (the rest)." Another prominent professor, when asked whether they took this stance out of fear or because they happen to think so, replied: "I think it is both – partly genuine beliefs and partly the compliance with the party line." I also think the same, but I do not give credence to the idea that the Kremlin's brainwashing is so effective that it can convince thinking people of obvious nonsense.

Thoughts are one thing, rector functions are another; the paths of reasoning of the same people who are both intellectuals and administrators can diverge radically. It required civil courage not to sign such a letter. The mechanism that operates in states that use psychological terror to ensure the public's obedience is working. Surely, this letter must have been slipped to the rectors by someone standing close to the Kremlin (it could even be some overzealous rector or a handful of them) and a list of those who did not sign it was automatically created. And almost all of the universities whose rectors are among the "authors" of the letter are state universities. At each of these, the authorities must care about the promotions of their employees, their salaries from the state budget, research grants, funding for equipment and modernization of the campus and investments for its expansion, diplomatic support in establishing foreign cooperation. It is hard to be an opposition hero when life's hard circumstances lead to cowardly conformism. The claim that an act such as this unfortunate letter can help "…not to forget about our main duty – to conduct a continuous educational process, to instill patriotism in young people, the desire to help the Motherland",[3] is more than doubtful. Let us remember that we can educate in different ways and with different results.

Notes

1. Peter Frankopan, "The First Crusade: The Call from the East", The Belknap Press for Harvard University Press, Cambridge, Massachusetts and London, 2012.
2. "Rossiyskiy Soyuz rektorov vystupil s obrashcheniyem" ("The Russian Union of Rectors made an appeal"), Ministerstvo nauki i vysshego obrazovaniya Rossiyskoy Federatsii (Ministry of Science and Higher Education of the Russian Federation), Moscow, March 5, 2022 (https://minobrnauki.gov.ru/press-center/news/?ELEMENT_ID=48060; access 05.03.2022).
3. Ibidem.

3

Nothing Justifies Russia's Invasion of Ukraine

Until the very last moment, I thought that Russia was not going to attack Ukraine. I assumed that President Putin understood that Russia would lose a great deal on the world stage from such an act and that he himself would lose the power and esteem he still enjoyed at home. I was wrong; I was not the only one.[1] It turned out that by failing to learn the correct lessons from the past, Russia can act as foolishly when invading Ukraine as the Soviet Union did when it invaded Afghanistan in 1979. Supposedly, Putin not only did not have enough responsibility but also imagination and, probably not fully understanding what he was really doing, he was greatly mistaken about the international reaction to his conduct. Yet, the supposition that he will lose power and his national esteem still remains to be seen.

Nevertheless, just as I assumed *ex ante*, I believe *ex post* that this mean act was avoidable. There was no objective determinism or inevitability of the military attack on Ukraine and it could have been avoided, although we do not know until when this was still feasible, and there will always remain controversy as to how this could have been achieved. The dispute over these issues is not only historical, as views are quite widely promoted that it will not end with Ukraine and that Russia may go further in its military actions. If this could indeed be the case, the question immediately arises as to what to do and how to do it so that it still ends up in Ukraine.

Alternative history—that famous what if…—is of great use in both economic analyses and political considerations. There have been several twists and turns in the past decade in both Moscow and Kyiv, and after each of them things could have turned out more or less differently than they did. It did not have to get worse at all; it could have got better. After the collapse of the Soviet Union, independent Russia—as strange as it may sound—pursued a policy of cooperation with independent Ukraine, but also of support for the pro-Russian orientation still present there, albeit subtly, without resorting to open pressure. And, perhaps, it could have gone on much longer. At the time, Moscow was still downplaying the claims of the people of Crimea regarding the annexation to Russia. Successive Ukrainian presidents, including Viktor Yushchenko (President in 2005–2010) and Viktor Yanukovich (President in 2010–2014), have practiced a policy of maneuvering between Russia and the West. It was not until the famous Maidan—the revolt and wave of mass protests in Kyiv's central square in late 2013 and early 2014—that the state of affairs was profoundly transformed and the situation changed. It was then—even before the annexation of Crimea—that Ukrainian policy took a sharp anti-Russian course. Thus, in the opinion of objective and professional observers, Ukrainian nationalists and their Western supporters have their part in the responsibility for how things turned out later when Ukrainian–Russian relations deteriorated more and more.

On the political side, I am close to the views of the French President, Emmanuel Macron, who also believed until the last moment that Russian aggression would not happen. Unlike the NATO hawks in Brussels, and especially his fellow leaders in Washington and London, he acknowledged that at least some of Russia's state security concerns should be the subject of serious attention and negotiation. Unfortunately, Moscow has most often heard that its demands are *nonstarter*, i.e. to be dismissed in advance—insane and out of discussion.

On the side closer to the scholarly narrative, I largely share the viewpoints presented by the eminent diplomatic practitioner and theorist, doyen of the international political scene, Henry Kissinger, and the prominent American political scientist from the University of Chicago, John J. Mearsheimer. Kissinger has repeatedly, and consistently over many years, spoken out against NATO's further expansion to the East and the idea of admitting Ukraine, a notion which particularly irritated Russia. It does not matter that we think that the possible accession of Ukraine to NATO would not threaten Russia in any way. What was important was that Russian leaders, and quite a significant part of the population, thought otherwise, and it was this aspect that Kissinger exposed in his position.

Although Russians were wrong about the NATO threat, they were given reasons to believe in it, which some of the more assertive, yet highly influential Western politicians now willingly—too willingly?—confirm. The UK

Prime Minister, Liz Truss confessed in mid-March 2022, when she was the Foreign Secretary, that the idea is that "we must also bring other countries into Great Britain's sphere of influence and draw them away from Russia."[2] On the same day, Jens Stoltenberg, NATO Secretary General, admitted at a press briefing after a meeting with member states' defense ministers that "For many years, we have trained tens of thousands of Ukrainian soldiers and provided large amounts of critical equipment to help Ukraine."[3] In turn, US President Joe Biden reports that US military aid to Ukraine in 2021—USD 650 million in the form of arms supplies and USD 350 million in additional aid—is "more than ever before."[4]

Ukraine's pro-Western orientation should not be synonymous with an anti-Russian sentiment. Unfortunately, this is exactly how the West has set things up, with regrettable consequences. Ukraine cannot have a good future without a well-ordered and stable relationship both with the West and with its large eastern neighbor. Now that the war conflict has heated up, this thought seems utopian, but time does—and will do—its work, just as it happened with French-Algerian relations, or with US-Vietnamese or Japanese-South Korean affairs.

One has to agree with Kissinger when he says that "Far too often the Ukrainian issue is posed as a showdown: whether Ukraine joins the East or the West. But if Ukraine is to survive and thrive, it must not be either side's outpost against the other—it should function as a bridge between them. Russia must accept that to try to force Ukraine into a satellite status, and thereby move Russia's borders again, would doom Moscow to repeat its history of self-fulfilling cycles of reciprocal pressures with Europe and the United States. The West must understand that, to Russia, Ukraine can never be just a foreign country."[5] This American statesman and realist warns that "To treat Ukraine as part of an East–West confrontation would scuttle for decades any prospect to bring Russia and the West—especially Russia and Europe—into a cooperative international system."[6] In the current public narrative, it sounds like blasphemy to call for Russia to be included in the international system of coordinated political cooperation, especially with regard to security. Well, there are such extraordinary situations when it is necessary to blaspheme and not to dress oneself up as a saint, when it is worth expressing one's own opinion, even if it definitely does not fit into the prevailing mainstream of political correctness.

Some authors dare to go against the current, but in accordance with factual correctness, with sound analyses, syntheses and conclusions. Thus, Mearsheimer argues that "…all the trouble in this case really started in April 2008, at the NATO Summit in Bucharest, where afterward NATO issued a statement that said Ukraine and Georgia would become part of NATO. The Russians made it unequivocally clear at the time that they viewed this as an existential threat, and they drew a line in the sand. Nevertheless, what has happened over time is that we have moved forward to include Ukraine in the West to make Ukraine a Western bulwark on Russia's border. Of course, this includes more than just NATO expansion. NATO expansion is the heart of the strategy, but it includes EU expansion as well, and it includes turning Ukraine into a pro-American liberal democracy, and, from a Russian perspective, this is an existential threat."[7] Yes, the NATO issue was key here.

However, the possibility of being a member of this military camp should not be confused with participation in an inclusive economic grouping such as the European Union, as belonging to it does not, by its very nature, jeopardize good relations with Russia. It is interesting and important that even President Putin put it this way, at least for some time, when he said that "We have nothing against it, it is not a military bloc. And we were never against it. We opposed the military development of the Ukrainian territory and had no objection to economic integration."[8] Sergey Lavrov, Russia's Foreign Minister, understandably takes a similar view: "Our position has always been based on the fact that the European Union is not a political bloc, unlike the North Atlantic Treaty Organization. The development of its relationship with any countries that wish it poses no risks or threats to us."[9]

Let us also add that true democracy—not necessarily liberal, whatever that means—needs not necessarily to be pro-American. Mearsheimer concludes: "It's not imperialism; this is great-power politics. When you're a country like Ukraine and you live next door to a great power like Russia, you have to pay careful attention to what the Russians think, because if you take a stick and you poke them in the eye, they're going to retaliate. States in the Western hemisphere understand this full well with regard to the United States. (...) There's no country in the Western hemisphere that we will allow to invite a distant, great power to bring military forces into that country."[10] This has been the case in the United States, at least since the Monroe Doctrine, so for two hundred years now. Can anyone imagine a hypothetical situation where the US does not take military intervention if some anti-American government in Ciudad de Mexico were to invite Russia—or China—to train and equip the Mexican army? And what if it had gone so far as to preach concern for its own security by installing Russian missile launchers south of the US[11]? Probably, the Mexican border cities of Tijuana, Nogales, Ciudad Juarez, Nuevo Laredo and Matamoros, and perhaps the entire provinces of Sonora, Chihuahua, Coahuila, Nuevo León and Tamaulipas would very

3 Nothing Justifies Russia's Invasion of Ukraine

quickly come under the control of the Yankees, as their southern neighbors like to call them.

While not denying that Mearsheimer's views are quite correct, it must be strongly emphasized that it was nevertheless the Kremlin's delusions and fundamentally false calculations about an assumed blitzkrieg that led to the widespread crisis with far-reaching and future consequences. It could have been avoided, just as its escalation and prolongation can be avoided now. Nothing justifies Russia's invasion of Ukraine.

It is not in any way justified by the otherwise deplorable repressions of the Russian language in Ukraine, particularly in parts of the country where it is the mother tongue for the overwhelming majority of the population. It is understandable that Ukrainian is the primary language in Ukraine, but Russian can, after all, function alongside it in administration, science, culture and the media, given that more than 17% of the Ukrainian population is Russian, and for almost 30% of them Russian is the first, if not the only language.

There are many examples of countries where minority languages are not only tolerated but even respected and supported—from Chile and Venezuela through Spain and Switzerland to Indonesia and Vietnam. In Finland, where Swedes make up only 5.2% of the population, Swedish is the second official language alongside basic Finnish. Every street in Helsinki has a bilingual name and nobody is bothered by it. In Poland, the sense of distinctiveness—in this case, more cultural than ethnic or national—is also respected, and in some regions of the country, official place names are bilingual, for example in Kashubia (Polish and Kashubian language[12]) or certain areas of Lower Silesia (Polish and German). The situation is interesting in some countries where the commonly used language is that of the former colonizer. In the vast majority of countries where such a language is English or French, let alone Spanish or Portuguese, it does not bother anyone, but there are also other cases. Sixty years after regaining independence from the 132-year-long French colonialism, Algeria's President Abdelmadjid Tebboune announced that from the 2022/2023 school year, public primary schools would move from teaching French to English as a second language, after native Arabic. In addition to the anti-colonial resentment, there is a substantive argument that English, not French, has become the global *lingua franca*.

Indeed, changing the name of the city of Dnipropetrovsk to Dnipro (interestingly, the province (*oblast*) can still be called Dnipropetrovsk) serves no good, and neither does the damaging 2018 decision of the Constitutional Court of Ukraine, motivated by nationalism, declaring unconstitutional a 2012 law that allowed for the recognition of a second regional language if more than 10% of the local population considered it their mother tongue. What is important, by overturning the regulations of the 2012 law, some regions in western Ukraine were deprived of the right to recognize the Bulgarian or Romanian languages used by the population there for years as equal languages.[13]

Notes

1. This was also the view of the then British Prime Minister, Boris Johnson: "On a visit to Kyiv weeks before Russia's invasion, Mr Johnson told Melinda Simmons, Britain's ambassador in Ukraine, that he thought Mr. Putin would be «crazy» to attack; that «he's got to be bluffing»." "Boris Johnson tells The Economist about his anti-Russia coalition", "The Economist", March 19, 2022 (https://www.economist.com/britain/boris-johnson-on-a-european-coalitions-role-against-russia/21808195; access 18.03.2022).
2. "BBC Breakfast", "BBC News", 16.03.2022 (https://www.bbc.com/news/live/world-europe-60746557/page/4; access 16.03.2022).
3. Ibidem.
4. Ibidem.
5. Henry A. Kissinger, "To settle the Ukraine crisis, start at the end", "The Washington Post", March 5, 2022 (https://www.washingtonpost.com/opinions/henry-kissinger-to-settle-the-ukraine-crisis-start-at-the-end/2014/03/05/46dad868-a496-11e3-8466-d34c451760b9_story.html; access 8.03.2022).
6. Ibidem.
7. Isaac Chotiner, "Why John Mearsheimer Blames the U.S. for the Crisis in Ukraine", "The New Yorker", March 1, 2022 (https://www.newyorker.com/news/q-and-a/why-john-mearsheimer-blames-the-us-for-the-crisis-in-ukraine; access 08.03.2022). See also John Mearsheimer, "Why the West is principally responsible for the Ukrainian crisis", "The Economist", March 19, 2022 (https://www.economist.com/by-invitation/2022/03/11/john-mearsheimer-on-why-the-west-is-principally-responsible-for-the-ukrainian-crisis; access 17.03.2022).
8. "«My nichego ne imeyem protiv». Putin o perspektivakh vstupleniya Ukrainy v Yevropeyskiy Soyuz" ("«We have nothing against». Putin on the prospects for Ukraine's accession to the European Union"), "Strana.UA", June 17, 2022 (https://strana.today/news/395943-my-nicheho-ne-imeem-protiv-putin-o-vstuplenii-ukrainy-v-evropejskij-sojuz.html; access 15.07.2022).
9. "Lavrov isklyuchil ugrozu dlya Rossii ot statusa Ukrainy kak kandidata v ES" ("Lavrov ruled out a threat to Russia from the status of Ukraine as an EU candidate"), "rbc.ru", June 24, 2022 (https://www.rbc.ru/politics/24/06/2022/62b597529a7947945743e69f; access 15.07.2022).

10. Isaac Chotiner, *op. cit.*
11. Something like that happened in 1962 during the Cuban Missile Crisis.
12. Poland recognized Kashubian as a regional language by ratifying the European Charter for Regional and Minority Languages in 2009.
13. "Rishennya Konstytutsiynoho Sudu Ukrayiny. U spravi za konstytutsiynym podannyam 57 narodnykh deputativ Ukrayiny shchodo vidpovidnosti Konstytutsiyi Ukrayiny (konstytutsiynosti) Zakonu Ukrayiny «Pro zasady derzhavnoyi movnoyi polityky»" ("Decision of the Constitutional Court of Ukraine in the case of the constitutional submission of 57 People's Deputies of Ukraine regarding the conformity with the Constitution of Ukraine (constitutionality) of the Law of Ukraine «On the Basics of State Language Policy»"), Konstytutsiynyy Sud Ukrayiny (Ukrainian Constitutional Court), February 28, 2018 (https://ccu.gov.ua/sites/default/files/docs/2-p_2018.pdf; access 15.07.2022).

4

The US Should not Provoke Taiwan to Declare Independence

As a man of science and a humanist, I live and still want to live in a world based on rational reasoning. Taking things rationally, something like a Russian–Ukrainian war should not happen. But it did. Should we then move away from rationalism? Should we accept as possible something that we have so far treated as extremely unlikely or even improbable? Should we reject rationality—in the third decade of the twenty-first century—and renounce reason for which wise men have striven for centuries? Not at all. But we need to have an even greater imagination than before. In advance, not afterward. And just as it turns out that one should have had more imagination before Russia invaded Ukraine, one now has to have it about possible, unfortunately, catastrophic developments elsewhere.

I do not think anyone allows the thought of an armed conflict between such current political, military and economic allies, and neighbors as Japan and South Korea that fought each other to the death three generations ago. However, the wounds of the past, when Korea was occupied by Japan and Korean women were sexually oppressed by Japanese army soldiers as "comfort women", are still unresolved. These scars do not allow the past to be forgotten and are still conflict-triggering, with alliance and friendship being enforced above all by the Sinophobia currently strong in both countries, further intensified by the US pressure.

Only recently—this time thanks to Russia's positive mediating role—has the years-long conflict cooled down and the fighting between Armenia and Azerbaijan over Nagorno-Karabakh ceased, but military clashes there can always be reignited, as it occurred again in mid-September of 2022, when at least 100 soldiers were killed. This is all the more dangerous as it could escalate regionally, which is even riskier as neighboring Iran and Turkey could become involved. At exactly the same time—in mid-September—dozens of people were killed in clashes on different borders between former Soviet republics, Kyrgyzstan and Tajikistan.

The situation on Morocco's closed border with Algeria continues to be tense in relation to the radically different attitudes toward the right to self-determination of Western Sahara. Algeria hosts hundreds of thousands of Sahrawis who escaped from Western Sahara after its annexation by Morocco in 1975 when it ceased to be a Spanish colony. Periodically, tensions rise, but fortunately, so far, there have been no armed clashes there.

Far from here, Bolivia claims access to the sea, but it is separated from the Pacific coast by the province of Litoral, occupied by neighboring Chile since 1881 as a result of the so-called War of the Pacific, *Guerra del Pacífico*, fought between 1879 and 1984, and a slice of southern Peru, the Tarapacá region, belonging to this western neighbor since an even earlier war fought between 1841 and 1942.

Relations in the northern part of the Indian subcontinent, in Kashmir, also remain tense. Wars and the legacy of colonialism have divided this 225,000 square kilometer mountainous area between three countries: India over 101,000, Pakistan almost 86,000 and China 37,500 square kilometers. None of these states consider the current borders to be undisputed and final. All three have nuclear weapons.[1] When in March 2022 an accidentally fired supersonic missile fell on Pakistani territory, Islamabad authorities rejected the explanations of the responsible India and demanded a new, this time joint, investigation. As there were no casualties, two rivals armed with nuclear weapons fortunately handled this incident calmly. The Indian Air Force said that the government had sacked three officers for accidentally firing the BrahMos missile—a nuclear-capable, land-attack cruise missile jointly developed by Russia and India. What if there were victims? If there were many of them? What if the missile was equipped with a nuclear warhead? What if it did explode? It is good that each of these countries is adopting a strategy not to use nuclear weapons first, but incidents do happen.

Unresolved are conflicting interests and territorial claims over the Spratly Islands in the South China Sea, which are claimed by Brunei, the Philippines, Malaysia, Taiwan and Vietnam in addition to China, which dominates the region. Taiwan and Vietnam accuse China of occupying Paracel Islands that supposedly belong only to them. In turn, the Senkaku Islands, in the East China Sea, are administered by Japan but are also claimed by China and Taiwan, who refer to them using their name—Diaoyu.

There are more conflicts—thus hot spots—of this type in the world, in several places in Africa, the Middle East, Central Asia. All the more one needs to have imagination while being aware of how political mechanisms work. At times, some of these stem from the fact that internal problems provoke politicians to distract the public's attention from their inefficiency to resolve domestic difficulties by stirring up old but still slumbering external conflicts. Demons can awake, or more accurately, they can be awakened.

A possible Israeli bomb attack on the installations of Iran's nuclear complex would trigger revenge in the form of a blockade of the Strait of Hormuz and then not only oil would become extremely expensive, even at USD 200 or USD 300 a barrel, but there would not be enough oil at all to keep countries, not only of the rich West, functioning. For many economies—and therefore societies, for people most simply—this would be a big problem. If this were to happen, we would remember gasoline at five dollars a gallon with nostalgia.

In particular, the US should not provoke Taiwan to declare independence. This territory with a high degree, but by no means full political independence and considerable importance in international economic relations,[2] plays a similar role in the current US-China Cold War as West Berlin did during the previous one, between the US and the USSR. Whenever either side wanted to slightly raise the temperature of the fortunately still cool war, the theme of West Berlin, which according to international agreements was not part of West Germany, appeared in one form or another.

It is not so much of a question of whether Taiwan has the right to sovereignty or not, but it is the issue of powerful China not accepting this possibility. Since they explicitly and consistently claim that in the event of a unilateral proclamation of independence of Taiwan—which they treat, based on legitimate historical and cultural arguments, as an integral part of the country—they will annex the island by force to the motherland, this should not be tested, but left to the course of things, i.e. the status quo should continue until a peaceful solution to the problem is found. This is what the wise Deng Xiaoping advised to do, saying that if we cannot solve the problem calmly and peacefully, then we should leave it to the next generation. Unless, again, one has to reject rational reasoning and write about the inevitability of the Chinese invasion, in the meantime, using the fight for "freedom and democracy", teasing Taipei to make a big mistake.

Quite controversial was the brief but sufficiently telling visit made to Taiwan in early August 2022 by Nancy Pelosi, who as the Speaker of the US House of Representatives is second in line for the US presidency after the vice-president. President Biden himself was more than dubious about the purpose of the trip: "The White House has been open in its opposition to any such trip, and President Joe Biden said the military assessed it as «not a good idea»."[3] And despite this, Pelosi landed in Taipei, further spoiling the already dire US–China relations. She said, how otherwise?, that her visit "honors America's unwavering commitment to supporting Taiwan's vibrant democracy."[4] The authorities in Beijing, on the other hand, reacted very harshly to the event, treating it as an American provocation. At a meeting of Southeast Asian countries in Phnom Penh, the capital of Cambodia, Chinese Foreign Minister Wang Yi described the visit as "maniacal, irresponsible and highly irrational."[5] It is not a highly diplomatic expression, as befits a head of diplomacy, but the substantive point can hardly be denied. In turn, a spokesman for the Chinese government described them as "extremely dangerous" and "accused Mrs. Pelosi, the most senior US politician in 25 years to visit the island China claims as its own, of «playing with fire. Those who play with fire will perish by it»."[6]

When such words reach us from Beijing, and a little earlier, on the day of Russia's invasion of Ukraine, we heard from Moscow that its nuclear arsenal was put on alert and that countries behaving unfriendly toward Russia could lead "to such consequences that you have never experienced in your history",[7] one can feel insecure. All the more reason not to annoy each other and make risky tests of the other's degree of resilience to political stress.

By the way, it is interesting that the Science and Security Board, SASB, of the Bulletin of the Atomic Scientists has not moved the minute hand of its Doomsday Clock after the attack on Ukraine and President Putin's irresponsible threats. Just as it was set at the beginning of 2021, 100 s before midnight symbolizing if not the end of the world then nevertheless a major cataclysm on a planetary scale, its hands were pushed further forward neither with the start of 2021 nor 2022 (the time on the clock is updated with the start of each year) nor after the Kremlin ruler's fateful actions and words. SASB believes that it had already anticipated this danger: "In January 2022 the Science and Security Board of the Bulletin of the Atomic Scientists set the Doomsday Clock at 100 s to midnight. At that time, we called out Ukraine as a potential flashpoint in an increasingly tense international security landscape. For many years, we and others have warned that the most likely way nuclear weapons might be used is through an unwanted or unintended escalation from a conventional conflict. Russia's invasion of Ukraine has brought this nightmare scenario to life, with Russian President Vladimir Putin threatening to elevate nuclear alert levels and even first use of nuclear weapons if NATO steps in to help Ukraine. This is what 100 s to midnight looks like."[8] Now, however, with the start of 2023, they will move the minute hand even closer to midnight. Even in the worst year of the previous Cold War, in 1953, things were not so bad; we were whole two minutes away from the "doomsday". Now, recognizing that President Putin is stealing tens of seconds from us with his adventurism, even if one were to accept that Nancy Pelosi's ill-advised visit to Taiwan and hectic Beijing's reaction to it have taken only one second of this so precious time, that is still one second too many.

If one were to assume that the visit by the Speaker of the US House of Representatives was indeed another step pushing Taipei toward a unilateral declaration of independence, one should not be surprised by the bellicose reaction of Beijing, which, after all, had warned of its unequivocal and tough stance on this matter in advance. If, on the other hand, Pelosi's less than a day's stay in Taiwan is to be treated as nothing more than yet another irritating US anti-China demonstration, then the immediate—announced a few minutes after Pelosi landed on the island and initiated the day after her departure—military maneuvers with live ammunition, including Dongfeng ballistic missiles, in the waters surrounding Taiwan, including areas it treats as territorial waters, was an overzealous response. This time it was Beijing, not Washington, that "played with fire". Just as an action provokes a reaction, overzealous actions provoke overzealous reactions.

Moreover, in the follow-up of the visit by Speaker Pelosi, China's foreign ministry said that the dialogue between the US and Chinese defense officials would be canceled, while cooperation on returning illegal immigrants, climate change and investigating international crime would be suspended. The worst has been the suspension of cooperation on matters related to climate change. Fortunately, it was only the suspension, after which China must return to cooperation with its adversary in the global climate crusade, which is all the more important that just after the unfortunate visit of the Speaker of the House of Representatives, the American Congress approved the largest investment program in the history of the United States, allocating 369 billion dollars to activities counteracting harmful climate changes.[9] Thus—this time very badly—the formally unrelated threads in bilateral political relations are interconnected, which in the case of Sino-American relations must have global consequences.

Care should be taken, because, on the one hand, more and more Taiwanese want their independence, considering their identity, after having been separated from mainland China for three generations since 1949, to be separate from the Chinese there. On the other hand, more and more of them fear war. According to a study by National Chengchi University in Taipei, when asked: "Do you consider yourself to be Taiwanese, Chinese, or both?", the percentage in favor of these characteristics is around 64, 32 and 4, respectively. The former group is therefore sixteen times more numerous than the latter. This must have serious implications. As far as war fears are concerned, there are certainly even more now than in the autumn of 2021, when, in a representative survey by the Taiwanese Public Opinion Foundation, TFOP, 28.1% of those questioned agreed with the statement that "There will be a war between China and Taiwan eventually", of whom 7.0% agreed strongly, while 64.3% had the opposite opinion, including 40.6% a definitely opposite opinion.

Care should be taken, because while social cohesion should be a feature of the people on both sides of the conflict—the People's Republic of China, PRC, and Taiwan—they are characterized by growing mistrust and hostility recently; the public narrative on both sides of the Taiwan Strait is not conducive to soothing sentiments and building peaceful attitudes. In sociological research, we have the right—at least in democratic countries—to ask about almost anything that interests us. However, in doing so, it is important to be aware that the very posing of questions and the subsequent presentation of the views expressed in the answers not only gauge public opinion but also shape it. This is also how polls regarding predictions of Taiwan's resilience to a possible PRC invasion should be viewed. Regarding the question posed by the TFOP in mid-2022: "Ukraine has fought against Russia for over 100 days. Are you confident that Taiwan can defend against an invasion from China for at least 100 days?", very confident was 17.2% of those asked and somehow confident 20.6%. It is quite a lot. But even more, by 13.2% points, held the opposite view; 22.4% answered they had no confidence at all and 28.6% were not very confident.[10]

Many Western politicians and opinion columnists being so concerned about the Taiwanese people's right to independence and democracy are far less concerned about the fate of other people who want it—from the Sahrawi in Western Sahara or the Issa in Somaliland, through the Palestinians in the Israeli-occupied West Bank and Golan Heights or the Kurds on the border between Iraq, Syria and Turkey, to the Assamese people in north-east India or the Papuans in the still Indonesian Irian Jaya. Some of these lands, according to the decisions of the United Nations, UN, should already be sovereign, in others, according to international law, there should be relevant referendums held, but this is not happening for a reason. Elsewhere, despite legal orders, the indigenous population, once forcibly displaced, is not being allowed to return to their native lands, as in the case of the Chagos archipelago, where the largest island—Diego Garcia in the middle of the Indian Ocean—is needed by the British and Americans as a military base. Sometimes, in an atmosphere of democratic platitudes, other people's aspirations for their state become simply a subject of bargaining. This is the case with the US recognition of Morocco's occupation of Western Sahara at the price of Morocco establishing diplomatic relations with Israel. This is the case with the political deal between Turkey and Finland and Sweden over their treatment of the Kurds sheltering there from Ankara's repressions, all in order to get Ankara to withdraw its veto on the two Scandinavian countries' accession to NATO. On the altar of its expansion, previous principles become shallow; in the name of its expansion, the distinction between independence fighters, who must be supported, and terrorists, who must be ruthlessly fought, is blurred.

Matters of nationality and statehood are extremely culturally and politically sensitive and prone to conflict, including armed and economically devastating conflict, as has been experienced many times on all continents, most recently in Africa in particular, where almost no border drawn by the colonizers in their time took sufficient account of the enormous ethnic diversity. In Europe, too, all legacy of the past is not resolved and the conflict-triggering circumstances are still lurking. Someone may ask: if Kosovars have the right to their own statehood,[11] then why don't Basques and Catalans have it? What about the Corsicans and Sardinians? Not everywhere, coming from different cultures and speaking different languages, it is possible to achieve such social cohesion as in Switzerland, where there are four official languages and, given the foreign immigrant population, more than a dozen are spoken.

One has to understand xenophobia, which makes itself felt here and there; people have the right to be afraid of strangers. It cannot be accepted, however, when in the social dimension, it turns into a sense of superiority over other nations, into nationalism, and even chauvinism, into hostility towards others—these strangers. The best way to counteract harmful and sometimes even dangerous xenophobia is to develop a spirit of tolerance for otherness and cultivate multiculturalism, which is by no means contradictory to patriotism and caring for one's own national culture.

Notes

1. The Federation of American Scientists estimates that China has 350 nuclear warheads, Pakistan 165, and India 160. For comparison, Russia has a lot more, 5,977, and the United States, 5,428. Along with NATO allies, France with 290 and the United Kingdom with 225 bombs, it balances the Russian

potential. Added to this are Israel, which has reportedly 80 warheads, and North Korea with 20 bombs. In total, that is a terrifying 12,695 nuclear warheads.
2. Taiwan is more developed than Poland. When counting in purchasing power parity, Gross Domestic Product, GDP, according to the International Monetary Fund data for 2021, amounted to USD 1.46 and USD 1.43 trillion, respectively, while per capita (in Taiwan there are about 23.6, and in Poland 38,2 million inhabitants) USD 62,526 and USD 37,786. These are general indicators, but Taiwan is relatively more important in the global economy than its 1 percent share in global output due to its position in the supply of high-end microchips.
3. "Biden: Military say a Pelosi Taiwan trip is «not a good idea»", "ABC News", July 21, 2022 (https://abcnews.go.com/Politics/wireStory/biden-military-pelosi-taiwan-trip-good-idea-87154063; access 4.08.2022).
4. David Molloy, "Taiwan: Nancy Pelosi trip labelled as «extremely dangerous» by Beijing", "BBC News", August 3, 2022 (https://www.bbc.com/news/world-asia-62398029; access 3.08.2022).
5. "China foreign minister calls Pelosi's Taiwan visit «manic», «irrational»", Reuters, August 4, 2022 (https://www.reuters.com/world/asia-pacific/taiwan-negotiates-with-japan-philippines-find-alternative-aviation-routes-2022-08-03/; access 5.08.2022).
6. **David Molloy**, op. cit.
7. To be precise, President Putin said: "Now a few very important words for those who may be tempted to intervene in ongoing events. Whoever tries to prevent us, and even more so, to create threats for our country and people, should know that Russia's response will be immediate and will lead you to such consequences that you have never experienced in your history. We are ready for any development of events. All necessary decisions have been made. I hope I will be heard." See: "Putin predupredil Zapad: Otvet Rossii privedët vas k takim posledstviyam, s kotorymi vy v svoyey istorii yeshchë ne stalkivalis" ("Putin warned the West: Russia's response will lead you to consequences that you have not yet encountered in your history"), "Vneshneekonomicheskiye svyazi" ("Foreign Economic Relations"), February 24, 2022 (https://eer.ru/article/obshchestvo/u64/2022/02/24/6823; access 4.08.2022).
8. "Bulletin Science and Security Board condemns Russian invasion of Ukraine; Doomsday Clock stays at 100 s to midnight", "Bulletin of the Atomic Scientists", March 7, 2022 (https://thebulletin.org/2022/03/bulletin-science-and-security-board-condemns-russian-invasion-of-ukraine-doomsday-clock-stays-at-100-seconds-to-midnight/?utm_source=ClockPage&utm_medium=Web&utm_campaign=DoomsdayClockMarchStatement; access 11.08.2022).

9. This program – deeply truncated compared to President Biden's original proposal – was approved by the Senate by 50:50 votes thanks to the decisive support of Vice President Kamala Harris in the face of such a stalemate.
10. "June 2022 Public Opinion Poll – English Excerpt", Taiwanese Public Opinion Foundation, Taipei, June 21, 2022 (https://www.tpof.org/wp-content/uploads/2022/06/20220621-TPOF-June-2022-Public-Opinion-Poll-1.pdf; access 3.08.2022).
11. Kosovo's independence is recognized by only half, exactly 97 out of 194 independent states – 193 members of the United Nations and the Vatican. Among those who still do not recognize the de facto independence of this small country (only 1.8 million inhabitants) are two members of the UN Security Council, China and Russia, and four members of the European Union – Greece, Romania, Slovakia and Spain.

5

The Fifth Partition of Poland is Being Prepared?

A German–Polish armed conflict—between two neighboring NATO allies and members of the European Union—is inconceivable, but how far can the deterioration of bilateral relations in the middle of Europe go when, three generations after the end of the Second World War and the political settlement of mutual relations, Poland or, more precisely, the leaders of the right-wing ideological and political formation that has been in power since 2015 are making a compensation claim for an enormous amount of 6.23 trillion zlotys, or USD 1,33 trillion? This is roughly equivalent to Poland's two-year national income, GDP, or 5.4 times of the government—state and local—budget expenditure in 2022. Compared to the central government budget, this is as much as 12.5 times of the expenditure. For Germany it is "only" one-third of GDP, but spread over many years—say 20 or 40—it would be able to afford it, just as it was able to afford the huge costs of reunification and the de facto incorporation of the five eastern Länders into the rich and much larger western part of the country, the Federal Republic of Germany, in the early 1990s.

Only that it is one thing to allocate even very large sums of money to equalize development levels within a country, but it is quite another thing to transfer huge amounts of money abroad for claims made more than 77 years after the war, and in a situation in which many legal arguments seem to prove that the subject of reparations should be declared closed. It should also be taken into account that some politicians, especially the descendants of those displaced from the territories incorporated into Poland, which is sometimes treated as a kind of compensation for the enormous losses suffered during the war, may wish to return to the discussion of the status of these lands (it would even be strange if this did not happen) and if not as much as to demand their return, then at least to strongly demand compensation—perhaps not less than the equivalent of 6 trillion zlotys—which the displaced persons and their descendants, some in the third and fourth generations, should receive. There is, after all, another similar case, which still has no end in sight, where the claims by the descendants of the Jewish victims of the war are addressed to Poland.

One may argue that these western and northern lands—also known as the recovered territories—are not any compensation forced on defeated Germany for its barbarities of 1939–1945, but reparations for the lost 175,000 square kilometers of the pre-war Polish territory to its east, which was taken over by the war-winning Soviet Union. Only that now, these areas are integral parts of the territories of Poland's contemporary eastern neighbors, Ukraine, Belarus and Lithuania, and probably no lucid person could even imagine trying to initiate a discussion about the possible return of these lands to Poland. Historical memory and historical justice are one thing, but imagination and common sense—also historical—are another. Where are they, when, above all, it is a matter of caring for a peaceful future? Unless…

Unless one assumes that absolutely no real financial compensation from Germany is involved and that the initiators of these claims are fully aware that materially they will achieve nothing in this regard. Being aware of this from the outset, however, they do so primarily for the purposes of internal politics. For it is difficult to imagine any opposition politician who, guided by reason and concern for the best possible relations with Poland's most important neighbor that are conducive to national interests, would be inclined to protest against such a serious political move by the ruling formation, which is carrying it out supposedly in the interests of the state and the nation as a whole. Now almost everyone is set in a specific way in the public narrative. No wonder that the Sejm adopted the relevant resolution with just four votes against it. Hardly anyone who dissociates themselves from such an unrealistic demand—which is in fact detrimental not only to Poland's international position but to the entire process of European integration, which just happens to be the best part of the post-war legacy—would want to expose themselves to an immediate retort and being named a "national traitor". Some, therefore, will remain silent, while others will allow themselves to be more and more drawn into an illusory debate that no one knows how long will last and which is actually designed to strengthen the political position of right-wing-nationalist circles. In these terms, such a move—which at the same time diverts public attention from other important problems, such as inflation, tackling of which is poorly handled by the authorities, the ineffective implementation of green energy transition projects or the dangerously growing imbalances in public finances—could prove very effective. For years, unfortunately, because during the term of the present authorities, Poland will not receive any financial compensation from Germany, which will be justified by those in power by the natural tediousness of such a process, and when the opposition one day finally takes power and gets nothing either, the forward-looking "patriotic" opposition will hold it responsible for the failure of the whole great political manipulation. The English have two terms for such moves: *policy*, i.e. intentionally rational actions subject to a substantive discussion based on transparent criteria, and *politics*, i.e. covert, deceptive actions lined with emotion and hypocrisy, often based on the principle of the worse the better. Poles have only one term: *polityka*. Unless there is a distinction between *polityka* (policy or politics) and *politykierstwo* (politicking). They should make such a distinction.

The Polish government, formally submitting reparation demands to Germany in the autumn of 2022, has not lost its mind completely, because, after all, it is not counting on obtaining any significant part of this huge sum. The Polish public has also no doubt about this. Having been asked the question in a representative poll: "In your opinion, does Poland have a chance in the future to obtain reparations (compensation) from Germany for the crimes committed in our country during the Second World War?", as many as 65 percent (27 definitely, 38 rather) answered no.[1] So why is the Law and Justice government coming up with something like this? Well, it is to further saturate its political course with Germanophobia. Russophobia was already strong enough before Russia's invasion of Ukraine, and after it, such sentiment is hardly surprising, while Germanophobia—an important part of the ideology of the nationalist right-wing party—requires not only reminding that Germany invaded Poland 83 years ago, but also convincing that now they want to deprive us of our independence…

Not only unwise but, above all, hugely reckless are the statements damaging to the European integration about the alleged "mortal danger" of Poland's joining the euro area. It is all the more astonishing that they are being voiced without any embarrassment by the head of the central bank, who should understand that Poland's entry into the euro area—obviously, at the right exchange rate to ensure that the export-oriented economy remains competitive—would be conducive to both sustaining a high rate of economic growth and low inflation. Adam Glapiński, President of the National Bank of Poland, NBP, a key institution guaranteed by the constitution to be independent of the government, instead of moderating his public comments and focusing them on matters relating to the monetary policy and the economic situation, for which the NBP bears shared responsibility, authoritatively states that "the idea is to implement the German plan – to overthrow the Law and Justice government, to establish some kind of «Tusk government» (because he does not necessarily have to be Prime Minister) and to bring us into the ERM II zone, i.e. to bind the zloty to the euro with a fixed exchange rate, which would be the foretaste of the introduction of the euro. After all, the official program of the new German government includes the construction of a European state. Something has to be the first element of this plan. This is breaking Poland's resistance, bringing our country into ERM II and moving us away from a radical expansion of the armed forces. Breaking Poland and attaching the Polish wagon to the German European train." And further: "For anyone who feels even slightly patriotic, it is clear that the zloty is linked to the existence of the Polish state."[2] Well, no. The Polish state can safely exist and its economy can prosper without the "radical expansion of the armed forces" and without the zloty, but with the euro, as long as it can pursue a strategy of sustainable development and skillfully exploit its geopolitical position, and not pursue a policy that is simultaneously hostile on two fronts—eastern and western. The conservative orientation and new nationalism make this impossible, bringing negative repercussions not only on the national scene.

While it is difficult to ignore public statements made by the head of the central bank, which are not only carefully noted by entrepreneurs, investors and players in the financial markets, but also by the diplomatic services of all countries with offices in Warsaw, it would seem that the pronouncements of a retired politician from the nationalist right-wing party should be quietly disregarded. Well, not if they are published in a conservative weekly, which is the only source of press "information" for an overwhelming majority of its readers. Loyal readers are not analysts who follow a spectrum of views, compare arguments and weigh up rationales; they mostly take the content presented to them at face value even when it is obviously false. What is more, the field of influence is increased when similar arguments are presented in other conservative-nationalist media (of course, they describe themselves as patriotic), which has, in the end, a considerable impact on shaping the views of a significant part of the population. What is to be gained by propagating such fancies that the fifth partition of Poland is being prepared? The fifth, after the partitions of 1772–1775, when Poland was completely absorbed by Prussia of Frederick William II and Russia of Catherine II the Great, as well as Austria of the Habsburgs, and after the infamous Hitler/Ribbentrop–Stalin/Molotov pact of 1939. Is it supposed to serve conservative American interests, which in a strong and united Europe see a challenge to US global dominance, or is it simply to divide the domestic political scene, as if it were not already conflicted enough?

It is amazing when the former Minister of National Defense (in 1991–1992) and Head of Political Cabinet of the Minister of Foreign Affairs (2015–2018), Jan Parys, writes that "Poland's full dependence on the EU is a condition for the return of the old balance of power in Europe, by which Germany, together with Russia, was able to weaken the US influence on the Old Continent. (…) Germany has been and continues to be an ally of Russia, even when it is at war. (…) The only way for Germany to continue its pro-Russian policy is to strike at US allies in Europe. (…) An exchange of power in Poland is being prepared and is to be carried out before the parliamentary elections through political pressure, propaganda attacks and financial blackmail. At the moment, the main force being used to initiate political upheaval through financial blackmail in Poland is the European Council, EC. (…) Overturning the Law and Justice government is not only in the interest of Germany. It is also a guarantee for Russia that the Russian–German condominium in Europe will return."[3] So instead of a European Union based on economic partnership and social cohesion, a "Russian-German condominium" is to be created…

To do so, obviously, Poland must be deprived of its sovereignty: "In 1939, Germany wanted to deprive Poland of its sovereignty by taking back Danzig and the so-called corridor. Today they want to take away Poland's sovereignty by making our country dependent on German puppets in Brussels. (…) In the twentieth century Germany, working with Russia, led to the outbreak of the Second World War. Unfortunately, as we can see, history has taught Berlin politicians nothing. Today, to continue their cooperation with Russia, they are ready to provoke serious conflicts with Poland and lead to the destruction of the current European structures. It is apparent that they treat both Poland and Europe only instrumentally, as a tool for their own selfish aims."[4] Such a narrative, which is detrimental to Poland's long-term interests, undoubtedly also stems from the fact that such anti-German resentment suits the US. By damaging NATO's political cohesion, they relatively weaken the position of Germany but also strengthen the Polish pro-Americanism, which at the current reshuffling of European geopolitics, is more important from Washington's selfish perspective.

Thus, Russia's war with Ukraine should supposedly be seen as a mere tool to reshape the European and, consequently, global geopolitical scene at

Poland's expense, which Germany, in alliance with Russia, has long sought in its interests. Such pathological views are not someone's private affair if they are propagated by public figures. This makes it all the more necessary to resist them, as they fall on fertile ground in a politically and emotionally turbulent situation. Some people can be really easily fooled, which may lead to even more serious problems than the ones we are already suffering from.

Notes

1. Social Changes Study for wPolityce.pl. Time scope of the study July 22–25, 2022.
2. „Trzymać wysoko gardę. Brońmy złotego. Michał Karnowski i Maciej Wośko rozmawiają z prezesem Narodowego Banku Polskiego prof. Adamem Glapińskim" ("Hold your guard high. Let's defend the zloty. Michał Karnowski and Maciej Wośko talk to the president of the National Bank of Poland, prof. Adam Glapiński"), "Sieci", August 1–7, 2022, pp. 18–19 & 21.
3. Jan Parys, „Niemiecki ambaras" ("German embarrassment"), „Sieci", op. cit., pp. 76–77.
4. Ibidem.

6

How Many Years Will This War Last?

Some, implying President Putin's intention to rebuild the Russian empire, like to recall his statement uttered in 2005 that "the collapse of the Soviet Union was the biggest geopolitical catastrophe of the century."[1] A few years later, as if to relativize that judgment, he nostalgically said not only that "Whoever does not regret the collapse of the Soviet Union has no heart...", but immediately added—in the same sentence—that "...who wants to restore it in its former form, he has no head".[2] Does contemporary Russia really want, just as Tsarist and Soviet Russia had wanted, to be ever stronger by territorial expansion?

Just as the suspicions and accusations promoted in the West about Moscow's intention to attack other countries in Central and Eastern Europe seem absurd, so seem the suppositions promulgated by Moscow about NATO's hostile, in the military sense, intentions toward this country. Neither NATO is planning to invade Russia, nor does Russia intend to invade other countries in the region. Even if in some sick minds in Moscow imperial fantasies of a Third Rome or a "Russian Mir" accumulated, even if the idea of attacking other neighbors, especially Poland, was dreamt up by someone in Russia—a view persistently pushed by some Polish political leaders[3]—the aggressors have already found out in Ukraine what their intelligence and army are worth.

In the current geopolitical situation, it is impossible to avoid controversy. This makes it all the more worthwhile to delve into other people's views when they are not the same as ours because there comes a strange time when it is often appropriate to doubt one's views. And so, one has to seriously wonder whether a ring of security or a ring of danger is being created to the east of Russia. "Central and Eastern Europe plays a special role in the US policy toward Ukraine and Russia. This is due not only to the location of these countries on the map of Europe but also to the experience of the Americans with the countries of the old Union further west. This experience justifies the thesis that, in the short to medium term (3–5 years), without dominant American participation, Europe is unable to build a significant and uniformly commanded military potential, which, in view of the real threat from Russia, will prove necessary in the conditions of the US-China confrontation. The Americans are thus creating a kind of security ring around Russia made of countries directly threatened by Russia and strongly motivated to make a defensive effort. This belt starts in Romania and Bulgaria and covers Slovakia, the Czech Republic, Ukraine, Poland and the Baltic States. Given the potential, Ukraine and Poland would have a key role to play in it."[4] If indeed Russia threatened these countries militarily, their strong motivation for the defensive effort could be understood. However, it is highly problematic whether such a threat is real or imaginary. Russia, on the other hand, considers the formation of such a "security ring" under the US control by nine, or more accurately ten, because Moldova must also be included, Central and Eastern European countries, six of which border Russia, to be a ring of danger for it; a knuckle rather than a ring. It will astonish future generations that in such a situation, there were no advanced negotiations held, no diplomacy to show off, no political leaders who could rise to the occasion.

Although promoting by both parties to the conflict of false perceptions about the aggressive military intentions of a partner, who thus becomes an adversary, is highly damaging to all the states involved, it is temporarily conducive to the objectives of their antagonistic policies. It will be extremely difficult to break out of this trap, as the language of cultural diplomacy has been superseded by the language of verbal aggression. How can we sit down at the negotiating table when Sergey Lavrov, the diplomat at the top of Russian diplomacy, is repeating the absurdities about the alleged genocide perpetrated against the Russian population in Ukraine, and his then British counterpart, Liz Truss, was spouting nonsense about how Russia cannot tolerate the existence of democratic states in its neighborhood?

How can a public dialogue be held if Dmitry Medvedev, former Russian President (from 2008 to 2012, Prime Minister from 2012 to 2020), writes on the widely read internet channel, Telegram, about what he believes are Russia's enemies: "I hate them. They are bastards and degenerates. They want us, Russia, dead. (…) As long as I am alive, I will do everything to make them disappear.";[5] How can a meaningful dialogue be held when the opinion-leading newspaper "The New York Times" publishes biased arguments of an American historian who states that "Russia is in the grip of fascism.";[6] According to Timothy Snyder, whose opinions have been eagerly repeated by the media in all anti-Russian-oriented countries, contemporary Russia satisfies the criteria of fascism defined as he understands it: a cult of personality around a political leader, a cult of those who died in the Great Patriotic War[7] and a myth of a bygone golden age of imperial greatness. This golden age is supposed "to be restored by a war of healing violence—the murderous war on Ukraine." And there is more. "Should Russia win, fascists around the world will be comforted." Probably because Russia is "fighting a fascist war of destruction."[8] This imprudent claim about the "fascist war of destruction" is worth as much as Putin's inane statement about the "denazification of Ukraine".

What is the purpose of such opinions? Well, to suggest that long war is necessary. Snyder's deliberations in the American newspaper are echoed by the British weekly: "Some in the West want a return to business as usual once the war is over, but there can be no true peace with a fascist Russia."[9] In passing, "The Economist" adds three more criteria for fascism: "a hatred of homosexuality, a fixation with the traditional family and a fanatical faith in the power of the state."[10] We might digress here that it would be enough to change the name of the leader, replace the Great Patriotic War with the Warsaw Uprising and the "cursed soldiers" and omit the word "imperial" from the past golden age, and his criteria for fascism would fit like a glove into the contemporary image of Poland. The absurdity of such a pseudo-scientific approach is absolutely clear!

Political clamor intertwines with media gibberish, making the search for a reasonable solution to the serious conflict immensely more difficult. The longer it lasts, the greater the tragic humanitarian impact and economic cost. The former—the humanitarian impact—occurs primarily in the areas of hostilities, but through complex transnational mechanisms also far from them, also by driving people living in countries affected by intractable food shortages and expensive energy into poverty. The latter—the economic cost—is still difficult to assess because while we know in principle how the conflict erupted, we do not know how and when it will end.

Before the war, Ukrainian food exports provided calories for 400 million people. In total, Russia and Ukraine supplied almost one-eighth of the calories sold on the global market. According to the UN Food and Agriculture Organization, FAO, almost 50 wheat-importing countries imported more than 30% of their wheat from Russia and Ukraine; for 26 countries it was more than 50%. In 2021, Russia was the first and Ukraine the fifth largest wheat exporter in the world, supplying 39 million and 17 million tones, respectively, totaling as much as 28% of the global market. If this is indeed the case, then the war in eastern Ukraine must have lamentable consequences in numerous regions far from the frontline. The land of these two countries[11] also grows a lot of maize and barley, which are used for animal feed. Ukraine is ahead of Russia in sunflower seed production and both countries—the largest producers in this respect—had 11.5% of the world vegetable oil market before the war.

Now, all this is a thing of the past, because as a consequence of the war and the sanctions provoked by it, all these indicators are lower, sometimes substantially. But the problem is not only that exports of grain and vegetable oil from the conflicting countries are falling dramatically. Another 26 other countries have placed severe restrictions on the sale of food outside their borders for fear of an insufficient supply in their own markets. There is a risk of an escalation of such protectionist practices, which may improve the situation in some segments of domestic markets and for some ranges of agricultural crops, but will worsen the situation worldwide in general, putting the poorest countries at a particular disadvantage.

The instruments used to restrict international trade in food are mostly administrative bans on its export, which in total cover 15% of the calories passing through global trade.[12] As a result, the number of people facing hunger is increasing. Already the coronavirus pandemic has caused an avalanche of problems in this respect, now there are more shocks to come. The worst thing in all this is that malnutrition or even starvation, sometimes killing, in this case, is not caused by an objective lack of food, especially grain and vegetable oils, but by logistical difficulties and political decisions that are taken so far from those who have nothing to eat.

The specificity of this war causes its humanitarian costs to be high. Whereas Amnesty International concluded through sound observations carried out between April and July that Russia had committed war crimes, it points also to the Ukrainian offenses. "Ukrainian forces have put civilians in harm's way by establishing bases and operating weapons systems in populated residential areas, including in schools and hospitals, as they repelled the Russian invasion that began in February. Such tactics violate international humanitarian law and endanger civilians, as they turn civilian objects into military targets. The ensuing Russian strikes in populated areas have killed civilians and destroyed civilian infrastructure. «We have documented a pattern of Ukrainian forces putting civilians at risk and violating the laws of war when they operate in populated areas», said Agnès Callamard, Amnesty

International's Secretary General. «Being in a defensive position does not exempt the Ukrainian military from respecting international humanitarian law».[13] Such practices are, in fact, the use of "human shields", which should by no means occur, and Amnesty International is right in saying that there is nothing to justify such behavior, not even the need to defend itself against Russian vile attacks.

The report irritated President Zelensky and caused the head of Amnesty International's Kiev office to resign. A few days later Amnesty International Issued a statement stating that it "deeply regrets the distress and anger that our press release on the Ukrainian military's fighting tactics has caused. (…) Amnesty International's priority in this and in any conflict is ensuring that civilians are protected. Indeed, this was our sole objective when releasing this latest piece of research. While we fully stand by our findings, we regret the pain caused."[14]

The statements on both sides of it are worrying. While those on Russia's side are not surprising in the context of its disgraceful conduct and while its leaders consistently speak of their conditions for ending the fighting, absolutely not allowing the thought of withdrawing troops from the occupied territories, those on the side of Western political luminaries must be thought-provoking. If former British Prime Minister Boris Johnson and NATO Secretary General Jens Stoltenberg say that the war in Ukraine will last until at least the end of 2023, this begs the question: is this a forecast, a scenario or a wish? If others, knowing that even if they wanted it badly, they cannot wipe Russia off the world map because it is too big to do so, want, in the words of US Defense Secretary Lloyd Austin, to see "Russia weakened to the point where it cannot do what it did by invading Ukraine",[15] this begs the question of how long the fighting is expected to last, fostered by the rearmament of the Ukrainians (most prominently by the Americans, with the UK second and Poland third), in order to achieve such a state?

Mearsheimer argues that although "Few imagine that US forces will become directly involved in the fighting (…) the threat to Russia today is even greater than it was before the war, mainly because the Biden administration is now determined to roll back Russia's territorial gains and permanently cripple Russian power."[16] However, it is unable to achieve this, so the situation has become a stalemate and an armed conflict under such circumstances not only has to last for a long time but also, even worse, may seriously escalate. "The maximalist thinking that now prevails in both Washington and Moscow gives each side even more reason to win on the battlefield so that it can dictate the terms of the eventual peace. In effect, the absence of a possible diplomatic solution provides an added incentive for both sides to climb up the escalation ladder. What lies further up the rungs could be something truly catastrophic: a level of death and destruction exceeding that of World War II."[17] While it is possible to agree with some of these general assessments and, to avoid the worst, consistently take into account even unlikely scenarios for the further course of affairs, hardly anyone would be willing to agree with suggestions that the "level of death and destruction exceeding the level of World War II" is imaginable. Here Mearsheimer is clearly exaggerating, probably wanting to stimulate our imagination even more, that although it is extremely unlikely, a nuclear Armageddon is not completely out of the question.

If, as regards the conditions for entering into possible peace negotiations, some Western politicians are making demands on Moscow that are even more far-reaching than Kyiv's—particularly with regard to Russia's withdrawal from Crimea, which was annexed in 2014—does this shorten the perspective leading to it or lengthen it? How many years will this war last? Will HIMARS, the High Mobility Artillery Rocket System, operated by well-trained Ukrainian soldiers, play a similar role in Ukraine as was the case with Stinger, portable anti-aircraft missile system, also supplied by the Americans, which in the efficient hands of the mujahidin in the late 1980s exposed the weak points of the allegedly invincible Soviet army? How long will this war last?

The Russians themselves have an interesting opinion on this matter. Less than six months after the start of the "special military operation", in the last days of July 2022, a Russian research group together with the Foundation for Urban Projects conducted a public opinion poll. To the question "Do you think that Russia should now continue its military operation in Ukraine or proceed to peace talks?", 38% opted for peace talks. On the other hand, when asked "If Vladimir Putin signed a peace agreement tomorrow and stopped the military operation, would you support such a decision?", 65% answered positively. It is difficult to assess whether as many as two-thirds of respondents would support a peace agreement because at the same time 62% believed that the "military operation" was successful (23% definitely, 37 rather). Only 19% (8 definitely, 11 rather) thought it was unsuccessful.[18] Maybe, it would be time to stop it because it was already successful?

It can be suspected that these optimistic judgments by nearly two-thirds of Russian society stem from their imperfect knowledge of what is really going on. Kremlin propaganda is doing its job and makes sure that people there hear about the "successes", and not about the fact that during the six months after the troops entered Ukraine, 70–80 thousand Russian soldiers were killed or injured (according to Western estimates, including the UK Ministry of Defense). Perhaps the decree by President Putin, announced on the first day of the seventh month of the "special operation", to increase the size of the army by 137,000 persons, will give them food for thought; that is twice the number of soldiers eliminated. The decree, published by the Russian President's office, states that "the numerical size of the Armed Forces of the Russian Federation should be set at 2,039,758, including 1,150,628 military personnel".[19] Such quantitative precision is astonishing and shivering. This decision proves that despite the setbacks and the rising costs of the war, on the one hand, and the increasingly felt effects of sanctions, on the other hand, the Russian leader is fully determined to continue his invasion; to the victorious end as the Kremlin understands it. So this war is going to go on.

Unless … Unless President Putin is removed from power not because of some great turn of Russia towards liberal democracy and civil society, which is difficult to count on, but as a result of a palace coup that will bring another autocrat to power, but this time an opponent of the war with Ukraine. Not even for principal reasons, but for common sense that Russia simply cannot afford this war and it is necessary to stop its downward spiral in the international arena. Seeking a quick end to the war, such a scenario would be welcome and at the same time, it does not seem utopian. It is utopian to believe that Putin will change, not that he can be changed for someone reasonable.

President Zelensky also changed his mind, or at least he places the accents differently than he had done earlier. Before, he looked for ways to end the fighting as soon as possible and start peace negotiations, putting, for the time being, the issue of Crimea aside. Then, less than six months after the invasion, he said, "Crimea is Ukrainian and we will never give it up. (…) This Russian war began with Crimea and must end with Crimea—with its liberation." A week later, on the occasion of the visit of UN Secretary General António Guterres to Lviv, he stated that any peace negotiations could begin only after Russia withdrew its troops from all Ukrainian territory. If so, then the perspective of peace is fading away. On this occasion, the media eagerly recalled the statement delivered a month earlier by Dmitry Medvedev, who said that any attack by Ukraine on Crimea would be treated very severely. While speaking in Volgograd (formerly Stalingrad), he did not mince words: "…some exalted bloody clowns who appear there from time to time with certain statements, are also trying to threaten us, I mean the attack on Crimea. (…) In this regard, I want to say that it is quite obvious that they have to understand the consequences of such statements, and the consequences are obvious that if something like this happens, there will be an immediate «doomsday» for all of them, very quick and cruel, and it will be very difficult to protect yourself."[20] Another second closer to midnight on the Doomsday Clock?...

It has happened many times in history that the wars that were supposed to end quickly had lasted so terribly long—such as the Hundred Years' War, or more precisely the 116 years' war which lasted from 1337 to 1453, or the Thirty Years' War of 1618–1648—that almost none of the warring parties knew what the adversaries had in mind at the outset, but almost everyone on both sides also knew that the wars had to be won. So, people were killed in great numbers...

Unfortunately, the war in Ukraine continues and the conflict is being prolonged. Six months after it was attacked by Russian troops, this semi-anniversary was celebrated in various ways, especially as it coincided with the 31st anniversary of Ukraine's declaration of independence on August 24, 1991. British Prime Minister Boris Johnson made another unannounced visit to Kyiv, while US President Joe Biden promised another USD 3 billion worth of arms deliveries (recalling that under his administration, it was already USD 13.5 billion in total). Speeches were made by the President of the European Commission Ursula von der Leyen (confrontational toward Russia) and UN Secretary-General António Guterres (more conciliatory), UN Human Rights Commissioner Michelle Bachelet called on the Russian President to halt military action, England's Queen Elizabeth II wished the Ukrainians "better times in the future", and Pope Francis reiterated his "invitation to implore the Lord for peace for the beloved Ukrainian people who for six months now have been suffering the horror of war." Thousands of press commentaries were published in dozens of countries. President Zelensky repeated that Ukraine would not rest in the struggle for the liberation of all its lands. In Russia, on the other hand, almost nothing; no special accents, after all, there is nothing to celebrate since the "special military operation" was supposed to be short-lived and victorious, yet neither the end nor the victory was in sight.

On this occasion, almost all commentaries—both in Ukraine and abroad, both political and journalistic, strongly shaping both public opinion and expectations—were quite unequivocal that this would be a long war. Importantly and interestingly, concepts, terms, designations are all blurred. Does war mean that there must be constant clashes of armies? Is war the same as armed battles? Are war and military conflict the same thing? If someone says—a British minister or a Ukrainian politician, an American TV station or a German newspaper—that the war will last a few years, do they mean the same thing? There is a strange consensus that the Ukrainian tragedy will go on for a long time, but there is no clarity about what is meant by the term tragedy or by the statement that it will go on for a long time. One gets the impression that for some observers—both passive commentators and those actively involved in the conflict in the form of supplying Ukraine with weapons and supporting it economically—the fact that this war will continue for a long time is no longer a sad thing. The question is whether this is an objective course of events to which one must adapt or a vision resulting from a consciously chosen geopolitical strategy.

It is not a matter of coincidence that on the occasion of the semi-anniversary and the anniversary, when an original exhibition of destroyed military equipment of the Russian aggressor was organized in the very center of Kyiv on the avenue leading to the famous Maidan, a prominent member of the Verkhovna Rada, Ivanna Klympush-Tsintsadze—former Vice-Prime Minister for European and Euro-Atlantic Integration of Ukraine—said that this war is costing Ukraine USD 400 million a day. It is not known how these costs are estimated, but let us assume that, in a comprehensive account, this is more or less what it costs the country under attack. If so, the first six months of the war absorbed USD 73 billion. In a whole year, it makes 146 billion. This is almost half the size of Ukraine's national income, GDP, which can be estimated at around USD 100 billion in 2022, assuming that it decreased by half this year, which is an assumption many analysts and researchers, as well as some national and international organizations, have made.

Ukraine cannot afford such a costly war; this context once again shows its absurdity. One can create illusions that the lion's share of this will be financed by foreign countries, but will it? Are those GBP 54 million (USD 64 million) brought to the semi-anniversary celebrations by the British Prime Minister (recalling that since the start of the invasion, the UK has already committed GBP 2.3 billion in the military and financial aid to Ukraine) and another American tranche, as well as smaller-scale Polish aid, as assured by President Andrzej Duda supposed to help? For how long, and how much will the foreign countries, embroiled in large budget deficits and an increasingly burdensome public debt and high inflation, be eager to subsidize a protracted conflict? How many more full anniversaries of 24 February would some declarative and genuine friends of Ukraine like to celebrate? Several? A dozen? Several dozen?

On its own, Ukraine is absolutely unable to withstand the war that costs it more annually than its annual national income. This conflict is turning not so much into a defense of Ukraine as into a war of attrition against Russia. If it is costing Ukraine USD 400 million a day, it can be assumed that it is costing Russia even more. However, for Russia almost USD 150 billion a year is only 8.2% of GDP (assuming, following the IMF's August forecast, that in

2022 it drops only by 6, and not by as much as 15%, as predicted in March, from the level of USD 1.78 trillion achieved a year earlier).

How many years does this war have to last for it to become, with the sanctions imposed, sufficiently devastating for Russia? The merciless economic and financial mechanisms of this destructive conflict work in such a way that Ukraine has to suffer a great deal and a long time, whose suffering is to be soothed, if only in part, by solidarity foreign aid, so that Russia suffers heavily, to the point of the suffering being unbearable. The problem is that, because of the relative size of its economy and its resources, the latter is able to endure for much longer. That is why this costly war has to last longer. That is why it has to be devastating. And that is why it is so much nonsense. Therefore, eventually, everything possible must be done to block its continuation and to find a peaceful way out of the impasse as soon as possible. Otherwise, the world will be setting itself up for a conflict in the East of Europe similar to the conflict in the Middle East over the Israeli occupation of Arab lands, which has been dragging on for more than half a century. That anniversary—June 6, 1967—55 years later, hardly anyone celebrates anymore. Another anniversary—of July 27, 1953, when the truce was signed in Panmunjom, ending the fighting in the Korean War that lasted from 1950—is sometimes recalled only by historians. The war on the Korean peninsula is over, but the conflict continues and there is no end in sight.

It is understandable that politicians have to make public statements, especially on such an important issue, but it is also obvious that all too often they think something else, say something else and do yet something else. In general, in politics, there is plenty of hypocrisy and cynicism, skirting around the truth and ambiguity. There are times when some politicians in prominent positions behave like show business front men (or even come from there), but in times of war, their public appearances are also the tools and ammunition of that war. Hence, there are many—sometimes too many—statements and sometimes they are not well thought out, but nevertheless, it is necessary and worthwhile to listen to them critically because they are yet another premise for deducing what and why things are happening, and especially what and why things may or certainly will happen. In particular, one has to be careful about the statements of ruling politicians. Many of them are shocked, and that is why they sometimes use very harsh language, because that is their substitute for reaching for tough measures—either in the form of rearming Ukraine or in the form of far-reaching sanctions, especially those that ricochet.

With all the West's boisterously declared unity toward the condemnation of Russia's aggression, there is no unity of opinion within the West on this issue, especially with regard to finding ways out of the impasse. While the NATO hawks want to bring Russia to its knees militarily, only some Western statesmen and politicians believe that it is more necessary and possible to end the war through a jointly worked out political agreement. This is because the most important thing is to end the fighting as quickly as possible so that no more people are killed. It is telling that after a visit with such an intention, among others, in mid-June by a trio of adherent *Realpolitik* leaders—French President Emmanuel Macron, German Chancellor Olaf Scholz and Italian Prime Minister Mario Draghi—the following day, British Prime Minister Boris Johnson, previously unannounced, visited President Volodymyr Zelensky undoubtedly to argue for his less peaceful rationales. Although Prime Minister Johnson collapsed shortly afterward for other reasons, suffering a spectacular defeat,[21] sadly his arguments take the upper hand for the time being.

Notes

1. "Tekst Poslaniya Prezidenta Rossii Federal′nomu Sobraniyu" ("Text of the Message of the President of Russia to the Federal Assembly"), "RG.RU", April 25, 2005 (https://rg.ru/2005/04/25/poslanie-text.html; access 18.07.2022).
2. "Kto ne zhaleyet o raspade Sovetskogo Soyuza Soyuza, u togo net serdtsa. A u togo, kto khochet yego vosstanovleniya v prezhnem vide, u togo net golovy". Interview given to Alexandr Zaldostanov, December 16, 2010 (https://www.vesti.ru/article/2072038; access 17.05.2022 when there were no sanctions blocking Russian Internet portals or it was possible to circumvent them using VPN). In this interview, President Putin quotes this sentence, asking to put it in quotation marks and suggesting that it was somehow his earlier statement. Some believe that he is not the original author of these words, but that he borrowed them from some other politicians or writers.
3. At one of the pre-election meetings in the early summer of 2022, Jarosław Kaczyński, the leader of the ruling party, Law and Justice (PiS), repeated the otherwise known opinion that "The North Atlantic Alliance will defend those who can defend themselves and at the same time have adequate resources to do so. These measures must be really powerful. We invest in the army so that in Moscow no one would think to attack us (…). They write about it all the time, they talk about it and hence the program. This is not our phantasmagoria, but an absolute necessity." „Jarosław Kaczyński: za naszych rządów Polska się rozwija i liczy się na świecie" ("Jarosław Kaczyński: under our rule, Poland develops and counts in the world"), „Polskieradio24.pl", July 3, 2022 (https://polskieradio24.pl/5/1222/Artykul/2992855,jaroslaw-kaczynski-w-ostrowcu-swietokrzyskim-transmisja; access 3.07.2022).

4. Andrzej K. Koźmiński, „Czy świat jest gotów na powrót Donalda Trumpa?", „Wszystko co najważniejsze" ("Is the world ready for Donald Trump's return?", "All that matters"), September 2022.
5. Dmitry Medvedev, „Medvedev o vragakh Rossii: «Ya ikh nenavizhu. Oni ublyudki i vyrodki. Oni khotyat smerti nam»" ("Medvedev about Russia's enemies: «I hate them. They are bastards and geeks. They want us dead»"), "Komsomol'skaya Pravda", June 7, 2022 (https://www.kp.ru/online/news/4778821/; access 16.08.2022).
6. Timothy Snyder, "We Should Say It. Russia Is Fascist.", "The New York Times", May 19, 2022 (https://www.nytimes.com/2022/05/19/opinion/russia-fascism-ukraine-putin.html; access 16.08.2022).
7. This is how the Second World War is defined in Russia, or more precisely this is how the period from the Nazi invasion of the Soviet Union on June 22, 1941 until the defeat of fascist Germany on May 9, 1945 is described. On the Soviet side, the number of victims is estimated to be around 27 million, the vast majority of whom were Russians.
8. Timothy Snyder, op. cit.
9. "A dark state", "The Economist", July 30, 2022, p. 15 (https://www.economist.com/briefing/2022/07/28/vladimir-putin-is-in-thrall-to-a-distinctive-brand-of-russian-fascism; access 16.08.2022).
10. Ibidem.
11. The share of agriculture in Ukraine's GDP is 12.2 and Russia's 4.7%. For comparison, in Poland, it is 2.4 and, in the USA, only 0.9%.
12. "A world grain shortage puts tens of millions at risk", "The Economist", May 21, 2022 (https://www.economist.com/briefing/2022/05/19/a-world-grain-shortage-puts-tens-of-millions-at-risk?utm_medium=social-media.content.np&utm_source=twitter&utm_campaign=editorial-social&utm_content=discovery.content; access 9.07.2022).
13. "Ukraine: Ukrainian fighting tactics endanger civilians", Amnesty International, August 4, 2022 (https://www.amnesty.org/en/latest/news/2022/08/ukraine-ukrainian-fighting-tactics-endanger-civilians/ (access 23.08.2022).
14. "Amnesty International apologises over Ukraine report described as propaganda gift for Moscow", "News", August 8, 2022 (https://www.abc.net.au/news/2022-08-08/amnesty-international-apologises-but-stands-by-ukraine-report/101310292; access 23.08.2022).
15. Matt Murphy, "Ukraine war: US wants to see a weakened Russia", "BBC News", April 25, 2022 (https://www.bbc.com/news/world-europe-61214176; access 1.07.2022).
16. John J. Mearsheimer, "Playing With Fire in Ukraine. The Underappreciated Risks of Catastrophic Escalation", "Foreign Affairs", Auguts 17, 2022 (https://natyliesbaldwin.com/2022/08/john-mearsheimer-playing-with-fire-in-ukraine/; access 29.08.2022).
17. Ibidem.

18. „«Voyennaya operatsiya» na Ukraine: otnosheniye rossiyan"") ("«Military operation» in Ukraine: the attitude of the Russians"), Issledovatelskaya gruppa Russian Field vmeste s rukovoditelem fonda «Gorodskiye proyekty» Maksimom Katsem (The Russian Field research group, together with the head of the Urban Projects Foundation Maxim Kats), July 28–31, 2022 (https://russianfield.com/nuzhenmir; access 23.08.2022).
19. „Ukaz Prezidenta Rossiyskoy Fereratsii. Ob ustanovlenii shtatnoy chislennosti Vooruzhennykh Sil Rossiyskoy Federatsii" ("Decree of the President of the Russain Federation: On the establishment of staffing Armed Forces of the Russian Federation"), Moscow, Kreml, August 25, 2022 (http://publication.pravo.gov.ru/Document/View/0001202208250004; access 25.08.2022).
20. "Dmitriy Medvedev prigrozil Ukraine «sudnym dnem» v sluchaye napadeniya na Krym" ("Dmitry Medvedev threatened Ukraine with «doomsday» in case of an attack on Crimea"), "Interfaks", August 17, 2022 (https://www.interfax.ru/russia/852578; access 10.08.2022).
21. It is rare in politics that the still-in-office head of government is referred to as a clown in the most influential Western media. This is what "The Economist" did, displaying its leading article on the cover with the words: "Clownfall: Britain after Boris" and an illustration of how Prime Minister Johnson breaks like a clown from the string on which he was suspended, practicing his political acrobatics. "The Economist", July 9, 2022 (https://www.economist.com/weeklyedition/2022-07-09; access 8.07.2022).

7

Against Whom the People's Anger Turns

It was impossible not to impose serious sanctions on Russia for what it had done. The question is what these sanctions are and why are they imposed, and exactly on what and on whom. In terms of crime and punishment, sanctions are a punishment for a crime, and as such some consider the wickedness accompanying President Putin's act of war, which he and his team continue to euphemistically describe as a "special military operation".[1] It is viewed quite differently abroad, where President Joe Biden was not the only one who did not hesitate to describe the Russian President as a war criminal.[2] Sanctions have their obvious political meaning; however, their key point comes down to affecting decisions.

In addition to the moral, legal and political aspects, the essence of sanctions is their economic severity and the aim is to induce the subject—person, organization, state—to change their behavior. This includes the behavior reflected in acts already committed as well as behavior implying an alleged intention to commit an act, such as, for example, the suspicion that Iran is planning to develop nuclear weapons. The purpose of sanctions imposed on Russia, its specific politicians and public figures, is primarily to force them to change their reprehensible behavior and to discourage any further bad acts. The question, therefore, arises as to whether the sanctions applied by the West are effective. Moreover, side effects of sanctions are important, including the ricochets annoying to those applying the restrictions,[3] and the repercussions for third parties, often far from the scene of the drama.

The issue of sanctions has a rich history, and thus extensive literature, which shows that they are most often ineffective.[4] More often than not, restrictions used do not result in the desired change in the behavior condemned by the one applying the sanction. Someone may cite the examples of the long-standing sanctions imposed on Zimbabwe and Sudan, which eventually helped to bring down the condemned regimes of Robert Mugabe and Omar al-Bashira. Someone else might refer to the fate of South Africa forced to abandon apartheid or Poland after the imposition of martial law. In all these very different situations, foreign sanctions have played a role in forcing the change in the situation as envisaged by those using the sanctions, but the changes occurred primarily as a result of other factors—the dynamics of internal reform forces and domestic revolutionary processes. These were the causes that brought down apartheid in South Africa and the kleptocratic regime in Zimbabwe, not foreign sanctions. They led to the political breakthrough in Poland in 1989 and the initiation of the systemic transformation, not foreign pressure. The lack of similar autonomous processes in other countries sustains the existing regimes there despite the restrictions applied to them.

One hundred years ago, in the years between the First and Second World Wars, only two out of nineteen attempts to use sanctions as a policy to impede warfare were successful. Two of these were the work of the League of Nations. The sanctions suppressed Balkan wars at the very beginning—between Yugoslavia and Albania in 1921 and between Greece and Bulgaria four years later. In the post-war period, an exceptional case of effective use of economic sanctions was the US financial pressure on the British pound sterling, which forced the end of the British military expedition in the Suez War in Egypt in 1956. On a comparative scale, there has only been one case where a country of similar relative economic size to Russia has been subject to restrictions to deter its aggression. This was the case in 1935 when the League of Nations imposed an embargo on Mussolini's fascist Italy in the wake of its invasion of Ethiopia. At the time, Italy was the seventh largest economy in the world, and thus relatively even larger than Russia, which is now only eleventh (in terms of GDP according to the purchasing power parity—sixth after China, the USA, India, Japan and Germany). However, the measures taken by the League of Nations at the time failed to stop the invaders and save the Ethiopian defenders of independence.[5]

Today, we can refer to examples of the ineffectiveness of sanctions against Cuba or North Korea, which have already been in place for several decades. The same is true of the several years of restrictions on Venezuela or Iran. The scale of these cases varies, the instruments used are diversified, but there is no doubt that they are economically severe and felt by the populations of the countries to which they are addressed. Yet, when it comes to the authorities, as Jerzy Urban, Minister-Spokesman of General Wojciech Jaruzelski's government, said after Western sanctions were imposed on Poland in 1982, "the government will feed itself". Governments, therefore, feed themselves, the people suffer, but everything has a limit…

The purpose of sanctions is to weaken and eliminate bad power, not to punish the subordinate population, often already gravely affected by bad governance of this power. Therefore, today, sanctions are more sophisticated and targeted, so that collective responsibility is not applied, but that they aim at specific spheres, places and people. Nevertheless, as time goes by, the ills of everyday life pile up—the lack of work and accompanying unemployment, high prices, shortages of desirable goods on the market, queues and rationing of scarce goods and services, widening income inequalities—causing people's anger. The key issue is against whom the people's anger turns. Against their own power or against those foreigners who imposed the sanctions?

In Cuba as well as in Venezuela, in Iran as well as in North Korea, the people's anger turns not against local governments but mainly against those who resort to sanctions—against foreign countries, against the West which, for all sorts of reasons, oppresses countries it does not like, as they hear about from dawn till dusk. Such is the state of affairs because, in these countries, the authorities largely, and sometimes even totally, control the circulation of information (and disinformation) in the media and are able to deflect discontent and hostility away from themselves, effectively shifting it to others. Anyone who has been to Tehran and Caracas, not to mention even more extreme cases of Havana and Pyongyang, could easily see how this socio-political mechanism works.

The Global Sanctions Database, GSDB, estimates that in the past seventy years, 1950–2019, there have been a total of around 1,100 instances of resorting to various sanctions, the great majority of which have proved ineffective. Of those in force in 2015, only 20 percent were considered effective or partially effective, which is most often justified by their proponents as insufficiently radical. In 2022, various sanctions mainly American were applied to 39 countries, of which 15 were African and 10 were Asian (including the Middle East). The GSDB classifies sanctions within three groups:

- first, according to the type, for example, commercial, financial or travel-related;
- second, according to political objectives, for example, policy change, regime destabilization, prevention of war or human rights;

– third, based on an assessment of the degree of success of specific sanctions from unsuccessful to fully effective.[6]

Counting since 1966, the UN Security Council imposed various sanctions 30 times on the following countries: Southern Rhodesia (now Zimbabwe), South Africa, former Yugoslavia (twice), Haiti, Iraq (twice), Angola, Rwanda, Sierra Leone, Somalia and Eritrea, Eritrea and Ethiopia, Liberia (three times), Democratic Republic of Congo, Côte d'Ivoire, Sudan, Lebanon, North Korea, Iran, Libya (twice), Guinea-Bissau, Central African Republic, Yemen, South Sudan and Mali, and against ISIL (Daish) and Al-Qaeda and the Taliban. "Today, there are 14 ongoing sanctions regimes, which focus on supporting political settlement of conflicts, nuclear non-proliferation, and counter-terrorism. Each regime is administered by a sanctions committee chaired by a non-permanent member of the Security Council."[7] Let us remember that the application of sanctions by the UN requires not only the majority support of the Security Council but the approval of all its permanent members, namely China, France, Russia, the United States and the United Kingdom.

Notes

1. Perhaps the first time President Putin publicly used the term "war in Donbas" on its 103rd day, July 7, 2022, during a meeting with obedient parliamentary leaders.
2. Interestingly, when President Biden, after reading his speech in the courtyard of the Royal Castle in Warsaw on March 25, 2022, spontaneously threw the sentence: "For God's sake, this man cannot remain in power", the White House officials tried to suggest that he meant something else than what was heard from their boss and by no means he called for a regime change in Russia. These officials did not clarify other words spoken by the US President on the same day. When asked by a journalist about President Putin's actions, he replied: "He is a butcher.".
3. For example, Renault's sales in the first half of 2022, compared to the first half of the previous year, dropped by as much as 30 percent, of which 18 percent was the result of withdrawal from the Russian market, which for this automotive company was second in the world, after the domestic French market. As a result, several thousand people lost their jobs in the company's French plants.
4. See, *inter alia*, Clyde Hufbauer, Jeffrey J. Schott, Kimberly Ann Elliott, Barbara Oegg, "Economic Sanctions Reconsidered", Peterson Institute for International Relations, Washington, DC, 2021.

5. Nicholas Mulder, "Russia's economic isolation will have dramatic repercussions for the world economy", "The Economist", March 4, 2022 (https://www.economist.com/by-invitation/2022/03/04/nicholas-mulder-who-studies-sanctions-declares-a-watershed-moment-in-global-economic-history); access 3.03.2022).
6. "Project The Global Sanctions Data Base", IFW, Kiel Institute for the World Economy (https://www.ifw-kiel.de/institute/research-centers/projects/the-global-sanctions-data-base/?cookieLevel=not-set; access 15.07.2022).
7. "Sanctions", United Nations Security Council, United Nations, New York (https://www.un.org/securitycouncil/sanctions/information; access 15.07.2022).

8

The Economics of Sanctions Work Differently from Their Politics

What is it like in Moscow? What happens in this vast country after the imposition of successive rounds of sanctions? Will the slowly escalating difficulties caused by them turn the growing public anger against the Kremlin or against the West?

Cutting off Russian pro-government media, especially Russia Today and Sputnik, from audiences in the West is debatable[1] because these (mis)information networks would not be able to impose their pro-regime propaganda on its inhabitants, while such a cut-off provoked an immediate backlash—depriving educated Russians of access to the BBC, CNN, Deutsche Welle, etc. It is a mistake to make it virtually impossible for normal Russians to travel to the West, blocking air connections with numerous countries where they could hear some truth. As a result, they are not confronted with a narrative other than the one that Moscow is stuffing them with.

One can understand, but not agree with, the rather naive call of President Zelensky that other countries ought to prohibit entry, except in humanitarian cases, to Russians who should "live in their own world until they change their philosophy".[2] Well, that is not the way. Those who survived a long time on the eastern side of the Iron Curtain during the First Cold War know perfectly well that traveling to the West was very conducive to changing the then-professed "philosophy". The best policy at that time was pursued by Western European non-NATO countries—Austria, Finland and Sweden—to which, starting in 1971, Poles could travel without a visa. It practically opened up Denmark and Norway for them as well. Therefore, Kaja Kallas, Prime

Minister of Estonia, is wrong when she echoes the Ukrainian President by writing on Twitter: "Stop issuing tourist visas to Russians. Visiting Europe is a privilege, not a human right."[3] Well, we differ greatly in these assessments, because the right to travel is a fundamental human right. From the dawn of humanity's history. European Union countries should not stop issuing visas to Russians, because such a total ban would be an obvious violation of human rights and a breach of the principles that guide democratic countries. Such an exercise of collective responsibility is not yet the biblical slaughter of the innocents, but it would not have much to do with decency either. Non-European countries, on the other hand, are guided not by ideology, but above all by concern for their own interests. Many of them, especially in Asia, the Middle East and Africa, earn a lot of money from Russian tourists. Vietnam, India, the United Arab Emirates, Turkey, Tanzania, and South Africa would not even think to give up this valuable source of income.

It is a fact that the extent of economic and political sanctions applied by the West against Russia is unprecedented. Such breadth and depth have never been seen during the last few decades in relation to any major country, let alone a military power, a permanent member of the UN Security Council, a major global producer of copper (25%), oil (12%), nickel (7%), aluminum (6%) and a significant exporter of natural gas and wheat (18–19%). Particularly distressing for Russia is the shock deprivation of the possibility to use almost half of its own foreign exchange reserves, equivalent to some USD 640 billion, of which more than half were located in sanction-applying Western countries.

But this time, too, the issue is multifaceted. Such a deed puts a strain on confidence in a global monetary system based on the primacy of the US dollar. Many people—especially in authoritarian countries, whose political and business elites may be concerned about how they (and their assets) will be treated in the future by the mighty that rule this world in the countries in which they place their free resources—will think that their foreign financial assets entrusted to central banks and foreign financial markets may also be frozen or confiscated by arbitrary decisions of the authorities of certain Western countries, above all the USA. They will therefore invest them in the currencies of countries that are not under American influence, primarily China, but also, albeit on a smaller scale, Switzerland, Singapore or the United Arab Emirates. This is already happening, as a result of which some of the world's foreign exchange reserves are shifting away from the dollar, against which confidence may be falling, to the yuan. Thus, its otherwise inevitable rise to prominence in the global monetary system is being accelerated. It is a perverse effect where sanctions designed to weaken Russia may strengthen the position of its ally, China, which may prove beneficial to Russia in the long run.

Analogously, in the longer term, the elimination of Russia from the international clearing and foreign exchange transfer mechanism of the Society for Worldwide Interbank Financial Telecommunication (SWIFT) may have a similar effect. This makes it very difficult for the economy to function normally, limiting the international liquidity of its assets and making it difficult to execute money transfers. Sometimes extraordinarily, because Russia—owing a total of around USD 40 billion in foreign bonds—although still solvent, faced with financial restrictions, was unable to meet its obligations for technical reasons. Thus, although it diligently transferred USD 100 million of interest due on two types of Eurobonds by the contractual deadline at the end of May, these could not reach creditors in Taiwan because they were bogged down by sanctions. So, although Russia has paid off, it has not paid out, so it is supposedly already insolvent. Minister of Finance Anton Siluanov described the situation so provoked as a farce. It is a bit like going to the bank with cash in hand to pay off a loan installment due on time but being prevented from doing so by the bulky donkeys, hired by this bank, deliberately blocking the entrance.

At the same time, there are works on institutional changes carried out, and Russia, under embargo by SWIFT, is resorting to forcing others to pay it in rubles or to use alternative settlement intermediary systems, including China's, growing in scope and importance, Cross-Border Interbank Payment System, CIPS. Cooperating with 1,280 financial organizations in 103 countries, by 2021, CIPS was processing the equivalent of around 80 trillion yuan, or almost USD 13 trillion. Now, in the wake of the embargo preventing Russia from using SWIFT, the position of CIPS will grow, which is something the West by no means wants.

It must come as a surprise that it took the West—led by the US and the UK, as they are the most affected—more than four months to decide to stop importing gold from Russia, of which it has plenty. It is likely that some of this bullion was also well-invested by some oligarchs enriched by thieving privatizations in the past years. They eagerly invested the exorbitant profits they made from such malpractice for many years in the West, again, especially in the US and the UK—the two largest money launderers in the world. The Washington-based think tank Atlantic Council estimates that no one keeps such large sums of dirty money outside their borders as the Russians—around a trillion dollars![4] Their transfer was carried out not only with the pathetic admiration of some media as to how much the yachts and properties they acquired cost, especially in London and New York, the French Riviera and Florida, but also with the awareness of local fiscal authorities and often even with the help of political high-ranking officials. There is serious literature on this subject based on sound studies,[5] but somehow bankers, lawyers and politicians have not been bothered by these reports, because not a few of them have participated in this reprehensible practice themselves. I have already discussed these pathologies several years ago showing how it was made easier for Russia's national assets to be stolen. Fritz M. Earmarth, a retired high-ranking CIA officer, wrote to me at the time: "American political and business interests got involved with Russian corruption and plundering from the beginning. It has continued to this day."[6]

Warnings of these foul practices reached the top of the political establishment in Washington but were ignored. Analytical papers and academic studies included statements about thieves' privatization, as well as the involvement of US partners in these "reforms" and the tolerance for it shown by the US authorities. However, the cacophony of neoliberal propaganda and, even more, the pressures of interest groups making fortunes thereof effectively drowned out these voices. The pathologies of Russian–American neoliberalism, warning of its dire consequences, have been reported to the highest levels of US administration officials, including the White House. Earmarth told me on the occasion of a conference organized in Washington in the summer of 1999 by the Jamestown Foundation that one important report came back with a handwritten annotation by the vice-president of the previous administration: Bullshit!

Zbigniew Brzezinski, an influential political scientist, also wrote about it and noted—putting appropriate terms in inverted commas—that the swarm of Western, mainly American 'consultants', who often conspired with Russian 'reformers', quickly became rich during the 'privatization' of Russian industry, especially energy assets.[7]

Now, even the foreign assets of Russian oligarchs are being confiscated—especially those famous yachts, of which we learn in passing that those belonging to the Russian rich men are as much as eight meters longer than those earned for, fairly of course, by the Americans (61 and 53 m, respectively). Such sequestrations are probably highly distressing for the Russian oligarchs, but it is doubtful whether they would want to topple Putin's regime because of them. It is also more than doubtful that Russia's foreign assets and the wealth of its oligarchs located there can be confiscated to finance the postwar reconstruction of Ukraine, as called for and naively believed in by some of its leaders and journalists as well as politicians and columnists in the West.

Its hypocrisy is visible on this occasion because it did not care about the issue at the time when the disgraceful acts took place. And now, under sanctions, the West is taking revenge on the Russian "heroes of capitalist labor", whom until recently it so admired and with whom it was happy to do lucrative businesses.[8] If these spot restrictions are well-targeted, if they hit those guilty of supporting the Kremlin's autocratic or hostile inclinations to other countries, then good, but it is not good if the actions have more of a propaganda dimension than economic sense. Another issue is the question of the legality of some personally addressed sanctions, as, after all, we have heard all along that private property is sacrosanct. Interestingly, it was also sacrosanct when it sinned.

Half a year after the invasion, we learn from the meticulous research of the British Royal United Services Institute, RUSI, that in 27 of the most modern Russian military systems captured, destroyed or abandoned in Ukraine by Russian troops at least 450 different types of unique components, manufactured abroad, mostly in the USA, but also in the Netherlands, Germany, Switzerland and Great Britain, have been identified.[9] The overwhelming majority of these components were delivered to Russian companies prior to the invasion, but on many occasions, their exports have still not been successfully blocked after the onset of the aggression. If this had happened, then without severe economic sanctions that would also harm others, it would have quickly turned out how non-modern and thus less threatening the Russian army is.

The economics of sanctions work differently from their politics. Sometimes surprisingly. One of the intentions of the sanctions was to weaken the ruble, which was to make imports more expensive and further increase the already high inflation rate, as well as raise the cost of Russians traveling abroad. Meanwhile, a remarkably simple trick—but how effective, from Moscow's point of view, to force, as it was described, "unfriendly countries" buying Russian energy resources to pay for them in the Russian currency—has drastically increased the demand for rubles. As a result, after a severe but short-lived breakdown in the exchange rate, when it temporarily fell as low as 150 rubles per dollar two weeks after the invasion, the Russian currency strengthened like no other during this period and its rate rose to the levels not seen there since 2015. On August 23, 2022, the ruble exchange rate was 23.5% stronger than six months earlier, on the eve of the invasion of Ukraine, amounting to 60.20 and 78.65 per dollar, respectively. At the same time, the zloty exchange rate weakened by 19.4% falling to 4.79 from 4.01 per dollar. Thus, due to the change in the cross rates, the ruble/zloty exchange rate strengthened from 19.60 to 12.58, i.e. by as much as 55.8%.

Paradoxically, Moscow has itself imposed "sanctions", only this time not making imports more expensive, but reducing export revenues due to the overvalued ruble; it was supposed to be very weak, but became too strong. Along the way, for those who can travel abroad—for example to Kenya or Indonesia, not to Poland or Estonia—traveling has become cheaper, not more expensive, as the sanctions were intended to lead to.

À propos, sanctions are hurting the mass of culture and nature lovers living outside Russia, who would like to visit this fascinating country stretching across 11 time zones and have not had the opportunity to do so before. Now, they do not have the opportunity to admire the beauty of St. Petersburg and the originality of Birobidzhan, to see the collections of the Tretyakov Gallery and the Hermitage, to be fascinated by the artistry of the ballet in Moscow's Bolshoi theatre or the opera in St. Petersburg's Mariinsky theatre, they will not see Irkutsk or Khabarovsk, they cannot sail on the Lake Baikal or fly over the volcanoes of Kamchatka in a helicopter, they will not see the beauties of the Lena or the Yenisei, they will not experience the hardships of trekking in the Siberian taiga or the Yakutian tundra. These are irreparable losses, or more accurately missed potential benefits.

The restrictions imposed on the ability to export a range of commodities from Russia are acute, the most significant of which are restrictions on the sale abroad of energy carriers—coal and, above all, oil and gas.

Motivated by common ideas, the West's intentionally concerted efforts to act in a coordinated manner in this respect encounter difficulties arising from divergent interests. It is understandable that France and the United Kingdom, whose purchases of oil from Russia as part of their total imports in May 2022 according to the International Energy Agency, IEA, amounted to only 13.2 and 3.7%, respectively, take a different approach to oil import restrictions than the one of Slovakia and Hungary, where these figures are as high as 81 and 64.4%, respectively. As a result of these discrepancies, the actual strategies of individual states differ significantly from what is politically and publicly declared as a basically common line. Thus, while in the half-year from November 2021 to May 2022, the share of imports from Russia in Hungary's total oil imports rose from around 43 to 64%, in Germany it fell from 30 to 23 and in the UK from 11 to 4%.

The partial embargo on Russian oil imports by sea to the European Union applies to a ban on crude oil imports from December 5, 2022, and petroleum products from February 5, 2023. The instrument to enforce compliance with these sanctions is making it impossible to finance or insure offshore oil transport until early 2023. The sanctions, however, contain some loopholes in the form of exemptions for oil imported via pipelines to European Union countries more heavily dependent on their imports from Russia, in particular Hungary, the Czech Republic, Bulgaria and Croatia. It is also against this backdrop that the intentions of the G7 countries—Canada, France, Germany, Italy, Japan, the United Kingdom and the United States—to introduce a cap on the price of Russian oil—announced with great propaganda flair at the beginning of September 2022—also as an anti-inflationary policy measure by slowing down the rate of growth of energy prices or even forcing their decrease—is seen as more of a symbolic act than a practically effective one.

However, through the complex supply arrangements operating in the globalized economy, the embargo limiting the sale of oil and gas from Russia on world markets—or, more precisely, on western markets, because not even in China or India—at the same time causes the price of these fossil fuels to rise to such an extent that, in sum, by exporting fewer barrels and shipping fewer cubic meters than before the sanctions were implemented, Russia's income from their exports has increased. It is estimated that during the first months of the war in Ukraine, daily receipts reached one billion dollars. In total, for the entire year of 2022 a current account surplus of as much as 265 billion dollars, the second largest in the world after China, was expected. At the same time, the mass of people in other countries—including those that have nothing to do with anti-Russian restrictions—pay noticeably more for energy, as it is based on raw materials whose prices are determined by the coupled global market. Rising energy costs are one of the main sources driving inflation, which in turn, superimposed on other inconveniences, is causing revolts elsewhere. Clear examples are Sri Lanka and Lebanon. There will be more to come.

Already in the first months of the armed conflict triggered by Russia's invasion and the sanctions imposed on it, serious disruptions in production and service cycles emerged in many parts of the world, but especially in countries with relatively strong economic ties to Russia. Germany, one of its main trading partners, has already recorded a case of trade deficit in May 2022, the first since 1991, when it was undergoing the shock associated with reunification. Exports fell as transport to Russia of restricted goods decreased sharply, while the cost of importing energy brought from all directions increased significantly.

Using the expertise of several European think-tanks and its own assessments, the European Commission estimated in spring 2022 that a sharp cut-off of Russian gas supplies to eurozone economies would entail a drop in GDP growth in 2022 between 1.2 and 2.6% points, which in countries with already low growth rates would mean recession; in 2023, this drop would be

0.5–1% points. In turn, the rate of price increases would rise by 1–3% points in 2022 and only very slightly the following year. And yet, prices have already been rising due to four factors: supply chain disruptions, adverse weather events, a new wave of coronavirus pandemic and a boost to global demand while the pandemic was being fought.

There are multiple deviations—both on the demand and supply side. For example, global PC shipments, according to consultancy Gartner, fell by 12.6% in Q2 2022 compared to the corresponding quarter of the previous year. To some extent, this was the result of a high base, namely increased sales in the two previous years when COVID-19 was raging and the demand for computers, especially laptops, rocketed due to the huge increase in online working and the extent of communication via the Internet. But above all, this type and scale of price increase is the result of logistical disruptions that have not been fully eliminated and fractures occurring in supply and production chains due to the pandemic. As a result, there is sometimes a shortage of components for production, which affects the relatively lower supply. This is now being compounded by additional cost-price factors, especially the acceleration of inflation due to the shocks caused by the war in Ukraine.

Notes

1. 70% of the population of the European Union are convinced (of which 43% fully agree), while 22% (including 8% completely) are of the opposite opinion as to the rightness of such a move. "Key Challenges of Our Times—The EU in 2022", European Commission, April—May 2022.
2. Laurence Peter, "Ukraine conflict: Ban Russian visitors, Zelensky urges West", "BBC News", August 9, 2022 (https://www.bbc.com/news/world-europe-62480087; access 9.08.2022).
3. Ibidem.
4. One of the staunch critics of Putin's Russia (and earlier, at the onset of 1990s, a supporter of President Boris Yeltsin's reforms), believes that of this amount, about USD 250 billion is money in the possession of President Putin's entourage, which in various ways supports his policy. See Anders Åslund, *"Russia's Crony Capitalism: The Path from Market Economy to Kleptocracy"*, Yale University Press, New Haven, 2019.
5. See, inter alia, Catherine Belton, "Putin's People: How the KGB Took Back Russia and Then Took on the West", Farrar, Straus and Giroux, New York, 2020; Oliver Bullough, "Butler to the World: How Britain become the servant of oligarchs, tax dodgers, kleptocrats and criminals", Profile Books, London, 2022; Karen Dawisha, "Putin's Kleptocracy: Who Owns Russia?", Simon and Shuster, New York—London, 2014; Filip Novokmet, Thomas Piketty, Gabriel

Zucman, "*From Soviets to Oligarchs: Inequality and Property in Russia, 1905–2016*", NBER Working Paper No. 23712, National Bureau of Economic Research, Cambridge, MA, 2017; David Sater, "The Rise of the Russian Criminal State", Jamestown Foundation, September 4, 1998, Washington, D.C.; Janine R. Wedel, "Collision and Collusion: The Strange Case of Western Aid to Eastern Europe 1989–1998", St. Martin's Press, New York, 1998; Janine R. Wedel, "The Harvard Boys Do Russia", "The Nation", June 1, 1998, pp. 11–16.
6. Grzegorz W. Kolodko, "Truth, Errors, and Lies: Politics and Economics in a Volatile World", Columbia University Press, New York, 2008, p. 238.
7. Zbigniew Brzezinski, "Second Chance: Three Presidents and the Crisis of American Superpower", Basic Books, New York, 2007, p. 64.
8. Six months after the Russian invasion, the 72.5-m Axioma yacht (previously called Red Square), was auctioned off in Gibraltar, where it was confiscated in March, but the money obtained in this way did not yet reach the Ukrainian poor. In turn, the American bank JP Morgan received a lot, since the yacht owner, oligarch Dmitry Pumpyansky—the owner and chair of steel pipe manufacturer TMK, a supplier to the Russian state-owned energy company Gazprom—owed this bank USD 20 million in unpaid loan.
9. Frank Gardner, "Tighter export controls on electronics could hamper Russia's war effort—report", "BBC News", August 8, 2022 (https://www.bbc.com/news/world-europe-62464459; access 8.08.2022).

9

Sanctions Are Intended to Bring About the Results Desired by Their Enforcers

As a result of the sanctions imposed, the Russian population was supposed to rebel. For the time being, however, it blames the emerging supply difficulties, high prices, limited opportunities to travel abroad and more modest cultural exchanges on the hostile West, rather than President Putin's regime and its policies. It is true that people are not demonstrating in front of the American embassy, but neither are they gathering with raised fists in front of the Kremlin. But this can also happen.

The withdrawal of Western companies from the Russian market is increasingly felt by residents of large cities (more than 75% of Russians are urban population). This will affect this largest country—stretching from Kaliningrad to Vladivostok, from the Black Sea city of Sochi to Petropavlovsk-Kamchatskiy at the Pacific rim. According to "The Economist"'s analyses of data from geolocation and information company SafeGraph, the closures of western businesses involve at least 3,500 retail outlets in 480 cities, including 1,200 restaurants and cafés, 700 clothing and 500 shoe shops and 400 petrol stations. In St. Petersburg alone, this applied to more than 300 different establishments that people with the right income have become accustomed to using.[1] They can no longer pop into Starbucks for a coffee, buy designer clothes at Dolce & Gabbana, are not able to go to the cinema to see a Hollywood film, and they have to drink Stolichnaya instead of Johnnie Walker again. Who will they be angry at? Critics of the exponential withdrawal of Western entrepreneurs under intense political pressure believe that this is creating resentment among the younger middle-class generation toward the West and argue that this may consolidate Putin's regime rather than contribute to its overthrowing. Others believe that the disappearance of branded, sometimes even iconic companies from the streets of cities radicalizes a section of the society and strengthens anti-Putin sentiments. How it will turn out, time will tell, although no one knows how soon.

To the surprise of many—some were very worried about this, others not necessarily—by the summer and autumn of 2022 the war was clearly dragging on. When it began, it was believed in Moscow that it would be victorious and short. This was also believed in London, except that they were thinking about a defeat rather than a victory, and they even offered to host Ukraine's government-in-exile. It happened differently. Putin's regime is certainly keen to bring the war to a victorious end as soon as possible, although the meaning of "victorious" is highly ambiguous. As for the West—especially the hawkish politicians taking the upper hand, from Latvia and Poland through Brussels to the UK and the US away from the front—one gets the impression that it is all about prolonging it because it is seen as the only way to defeat Russia. It is the Ukrainians who suffer the most from such prolongation; according to the Kyiv authorities, around two hundred Ukrainians have been killed every day during the ongoing fighting and many thousands are suffering. The absurdity of this war is perhaps also shown by "The Economist" when it writes: "Even if lost territory will be hard to retake [through prolonging this war], Ukraine can demonstrate the futility of Vladimir Putin's campaign and emerge as a democratic, Westward-looking state."[2] The state of affairs, which a prominent Ukrainian economist describes as a hybrid "peace-war" system, will therefore persist.[3]

No one knows for sure how long such a state of affairs can last, but it will certainly continue long enough to complicate international relations even more than they already are. In May 2022, Henry Kissinger warned of such consequences in a speech (online) at the World Economic Forum in Davos, saying that "The most vivid at the moment is the war in Ukraine, and the outcome of that war, both in the military and political sense, will affect relations between groupings of countries. (…) And the outcome of any war and the peace settlement, and the nature of that peace settlement—it will determine whether the combatants remain permanent adversaries, or whether it is possible to fit them into an international framework".[4] Drawing on his political and diplomatic experience from the Vietnam War, which ended half a century ago, and the ongoing Israeli–Palestinian conflict in the Middle East, Kissinger suggests that stopping the exhausting fighting and entering into peace negotiations as soon as possible is worth even the territorial concessions in the eastern Donbas to Russia. Few people share such a pragmatic but hard-to-digest point of view, so the clashes continue.

Against this backdrop, the comment made by the governor of the Lugansk region following the withdrawal of Ukrainian troops from Sevrodonetsk, which was besieged by Russian troops, was telling: "Remaining in positions that have been relentlessly shelled for months just doesn't make sense."[5] He said that exactly four months after the outbreak of the war, when "The city's entire infrastructure has been completely destroyed, with over 90% of houses shelled and 80% of them critically damaged."[6] Others believe that it makes total sense to remain in position for as long as possible—until victory, even if it should not come and even if not one stone is left standing upon another…

Sanctions are intended to bring about the results desired by their enforcers but to do so, they must last for a long time. In turn, for their long duration to be justified, the conflict must last for a long time, as well. Yet, sanctions may have a perverse effect. In the long term, their economic aspect may prove beneficial to Russia, as the restrictions applied force it to diversify its economy. So far, it has been quasi-monocultural, with a huge—and unhealthy for sustainability—importance of raw materials sectors, especially fossil fuels. Now, under external coercion, Russians will have to liberate themselves from the domination of this resource curse and learn to produce a variety of goods and provide various services that are subject to partial or full embargo. Sometimes it comes very easily and quickly, when after just a few months, instead of the American restaurant chain McDonald's there is their own, "Vkusno i tochka", i.e. "Tasty and that's it", or Coffee Star instead of Starbucks, with a very similar logo depicting a woman's head in the center of a circle, but wearing a traditional Russian headdress. At other times it must take a long time and is unlikely to be fully successful, as in the case of replacing BMW with its own manufacture, when they withdrew from both the supply of finished cars and their assembly in Russia. Yet, at other times it may not succeed at all, if only with regard to the production of high-end computer chips.

The political aspect of the possible perverse effect of the sanctions would undermine their sense altogether. The anti-Western sentiments among the Russian public during the first period of sanctions are favorable rather than harmful to Putin's regime. And in the long term, when restrictions that annoy the people result in public demonstrations of their discontent, the authorities may further tighten their already considerable scope of control of the society. Consequently, instead of the desired by the West evolution toward liberal democracy and civil society, Russia may move even further toward an authoritarian system. No doubt, this will be justified by the Kremlin and its supporters in the media—and, unfortunately, also in the supposedly scholarly arguments of the social sciences—as a legitimate response to the West's hostility motivated by its anti-Russian orientation. Signs of such evolution can already be seen.

Likewise, the same is happening in China, where Xi Jinping's authoritarian regime is lengthening as the party leader and state president can now rule indefinitely. Over the past four decades, his predecessors honored the principle of party leadership and the highest state office for no more than two terms. Now, the more critical—or, according to Beijing, hostile—the attitude of foreign countries towards China, the more authoritarianism is exacerbated. The more the West supports pluralism and civil liberties in China, the less Chinese people can enjoy them. There is also less free public discussion because the monoparty authorities see it as a threat to their omnipotence. Even in the community of social sciences, there is less tolerance for unorthodox thoughts than before.

Putin's regime has already had many of the hallmarks of authoritarianism before the invasion, which an increasing number of experts on the issue describe as new, distinguishing it from the old. Several of its features are pointed out. Thus, "First, new authoritarian regimes are based on basically free (if not always fair) elections, in which rulers receive and renew their mandate in an open competition. The political opposition not only exists but has the possibility to compete in elections. Support for the regime is so strong that there is no need to steal elections; at the worst, there might be some manipulation with the results, but not to the extent which would make elections meaningless. (…) Second, political pluralism exists and is reflected in the existence of political parties and associations as well as in the media. The regime controls public media, but there is plenty of room for independent channels, including the Internet. Third, new authoritarianism uses the coercive measures, but does it in a less flagrant way than old authoritarianism, except in conditions of acute crisis. (…) Fourth, in most of the authoritarian regimes of the past, the armed forces were either in power or constituted a very important part of the ruling bloc (like in Poland, 1926–1939 or in Spain, 1939–1975). New authoritarianism is based on civilian control of the armed forces and—while supported by the military—does not depend on them for staying in power."[7] Well, that's it; we already have "conditions of acute crisis", so it is to be expected that the coercive measures will also become increasingly severe. We already know that they are.

What we do not know, however, and what only time will show, is how long Russia's new authoritarianism headed by Putin will last. Will the attack on Ukraine weaken or strengthen it? Before the aggression, it was believed that "As a model of new authoritarianism, Putin's regime can last a long time and inspires replication in several other former Soviet republics, particularly in Central Asia. Its future depends on the ability to meet the expectations of continuous economic improvement and of maintaining Russia's position as one of the major regional powers."[8] But right now, this regime is not conducive to maintaining Russia's international position, and it certainly will not be able to live up to the "expectations of continued economic improvement", because the economic situation—before it ever starts to improve again—will first deteriorate severely.

While sanctions are a serious matter, there are plenty of questionable or even frivolous behaviors. Emotions work—often more than reason—and as a result, for example, Russian cats are banned from participating in European beauty contests. Russian athletes are de facto being harassed by being prevented from taking part in numerous competitions for which they have been painstakingly preparing for years. Rarely are such calm and principled responses made as in the case of the reaction of relevant Nepalese authorities, who replied to Ukraine's wish to ban Russian Himalayan climbers from the highest peaks: "We believe our mountains are global assets and any countries' citizens willing to visit them for attainment of peace should be allowed to do so – as long as they do it within our legal provisions."[9]

New York's Metropolitan Opera broke its contract with Anna Netrebko and now someone else, not necessarily as magnificent as she is, must sing the part of Lady Macbeth in Verdi's opera there. In the USA and Western Europe, contracts with Valery Gergiev, the world's most eminent contemporary conductor, were broken. Some directors of music and theatre stages make fools of themselves when they remove such masterpieces as "Eugene Onegin", composed by Pyotr Tchaikovsky (1840–1893) to a libretto by an even earlier author, Alexander Pushkin (1799–1837), from the opera repertoire, or they delete from the philharmonic program the works by Sergei Rachmaninoff (1873–1943), who happened to have left Russia for the West immediately after the outbreak of the Bolshevik Revolution in 1918, or get off the stage a drama by Nikolai Gogol (1809–1852), who actually embodied Russian-Ukrainian cultural identity. All this is happening, so to say, on the margins of big issues but such excesses should not be taken lightly, as they limit cultural, scientific and sporting exchanges, which are supposed to be about building bridges between nations, not walls separating them. Equally important is that the Kremlin will definitely use such excesses against the West, which is so fond of emphasizing that it is guided by culture, integrity and recognized rules of conduct in international relations.

Ukrainian economists must reluctantly accept the fact that overzealous government decisions made earlier, in 2020–2021, have already banned publishing in Russian—the language spoken professionally by most of them—from scientific periodicals such as "Ekonomika Ukrainy" or "Ekonomichna Teoriya, sponsored by the National Academy of Science of Ukraine. At first, the ban covered only printed editions, then also electronic ones.

Ukrainian parliamentarians could not bear the tension anymore, as well, and in the fourth month of the armed conflict passed a law banning the public display of Russian songs. A peculiar law of the Verkhovna Rada, the Ukrainian Parliament, prohibits public performances on the territory of Ukraine and bans "making public by any means of communication (…) phonograms, videograms and music clips containing a recorded performance of a non-dramatic musical work with lyrics written by a singer (male or female) who is or was at any time after 1991 a citizen of a state recognized by the Verkhovna Rada of Ukraine as an aggressor state."[10] This piece of legislation was adopted by 330 votes with no oppositions or abstentions. I do not think unanimity can be that mindless. Those thinking differently in this vote (and other votes with similar results) rather do not dare to show their views because they are so mentally terrorized by the storm of politicians' narratives and media turmoil that they vote not as they think, but as they need to. Lucky are the artists who died during the USSR times because they are not affected by it; it is different for those who survived its collapse. Will then the broadcasting of Alla Pugacheva's songs or Buat Okudzhava's ballads by independent radio be punishable by fines or even worse? The former, in order to be allowed to be listened to, can still make a statement condemning the transgression of its president, the latter cannot because he is no longer with us for years, but his poetry and music are. Banning such works cannot evoke good memories.

Notes

1. "Western firms' thorny Russian dilemma", "The Economist", March 19, 2022 (https://www.economist.com/business/western-firms-thorny-russian-dilemmas/21808196; access 23.03.2022).
2. "How to win Ukraine's long war", "The Economist", June 30, 2022 (https://www.economist.com/leaders/2022/06/30/how-to-win-ukraines-long-war; access 2.07.2022).

3. Andrii Grytsenko, "Hybrid System «Peace-War» as a Modern Form of the Changing World Order", in: Andrii Grytsenko, Merve Kidiryuz (eds.), "Proceeding Book: 2. International Symposium on War Studies", 20–21 May, 2022, Ankara, pp. 67–73 (https://www.izdas.org/_files/ugd/262ebf_c81b06 74b9774454af80bdb40bc70421.pdf; access 12.07.2022).
4. Henry Kissinger, "These are the main geopolitical challenges facing the world right now", World Economic Forum, Annual Meeting 2022, May 23, 2022 (https://www.weforum.org/agenda/2022/05/kissinger-these-are-the-main-geo political-challenges-facing-the-world-right-now/; access 31.07.2022).
5. "Ukraine war: Kyiv orders forces to withdraw from Severodonetsk", "BBC News", June 24, 2022 (https://www.bbc.com/news/world-europe-61920708; access 2.08.2022).
6. Ibidem.
7. Jerzy J. Wiatr (ed.), "New Authoritarianism: Challenges to Democracy in the 21st Century", Verlag Barbara Budrich, Opladen—Berlin—Toronto, 2019, pp. 173–174.
8. Jerzy J. Wiatr, "Political Leadership: Between Democracy and Authoritarianism", Barbara Budrich Publishers, Opladen—Berlin—Toronto, 2021, p. 162.
9. Navin Singh Khadka, "Ukraine calls for Nepal to ban Russian climbers from Himalayas", "BBC News", 29.03.2022 (https://www.bbc.com/news/world-asia-60915320; access 30.03.2022).
10. "Proekt Zakonu pro vnesennya zmin do deyakykh zakoniv Ukrayiny shchodo pidtrymky natsional′noho muzychnoho produktu ta obmezhennya publichnoho vykorystannya muzychnoho produktu derzhavy-ahresora" ("Draft Law on Amendments to Certain Laws of Ukraine Regarding Support of the National Musical Product and Restriction of Public Use of the Musical Product of the Aggressor State"), Verkhovna Rada Ukrayiny (Verkhovna Rada of Ukraine), 19.06.2022 (https://itd.rada.gov.ua/billInfo/Bills/Card/39702; access 3.07.2022).

10

Great Inflation Is a Delayed Invoice for the Pandemic and a Prepayment for the War

The current process of rising price levels is specific in that it is due to a combination of supply and demand causes, and is further driven by inflationary expectations. The last factor of a psychological nature is of particular importance in circumstances of the unstable social and political situation, when people, expecting further price increases or shortages of goods on the market, buy in excess of their current needs. As a result, an additional increase in demand causes an additional increase in prices. Producers, suppliers and sellers are also raising them in anticipation of further inflationary growth in demand. The bigger the eyes inflation has in human perception and expectations about its level in the future, the higher this level becomes.

One might say that the current inflation is nothing new; everything was already there. After all, to counteract it one must rely on the ability to twist the head of the hydra. And it has many heads. This time, the great inflation is a delayed invoice for the pandemic and a prepayment for the war. Its uniqueness derives from the fact that it is both a delayed bill to pay for the expenses incurred in the fight against the pandemic—when, following the "printing" of money without coverage in the mass of goods and services, prices rose insufficiently fast from the point of view of market equilibrium and a prepayment for the costs that will have to be paid by the end of the war in Ukraine and its international aftermath. These shocks in particular are used in attempts to explain the major acceleration of inflation in 2022. This is done not only by governments and central banks, which in doing so wish to shift as much responsibility as possible away from themselves for the high inflation rate to which they have contributed with their errors committed in revenue, fiscal and monetary policy but also by pro-government economists.

The Polish public opinion sets the responsibility for inflation in interesting proportions. To the question asked in a survey conducted in early July 2022, "Who or what do you think is most responsible for the current price increase?", six answer options were suggested: (1) Increase in energy and fuel prices due to the war in Ukraine, (2) Government policy, (3) Consequences of the COVID-19 pandemic and its management, (4) EU climate policy, (5) None of these, and (6) I don't know, it's hard to say. Probably by managing the pandemic, the questioner understood the government's policy of counteracting it, and directing the attention to the European Union regarding climate policy had been intended to divert attention from the responsibility of national policies regarding the situation in this area. Two-thirds, respectively 33.3 and 33.7%, respondents opted for factors (1) and (2) as the biggest culprits. Factor (3) obtained 14.1 and (4) 9.6% of the votes. Factor (5) was chosen by 1.5 and (6) by 7.8% of the respondents.[1] Thus, as much as 42.9% of them see the causes of inflation outside, in the effects of the Russian invasion of Ukraine (hence the term "Putinflation" promoted in journalism) and in the EU climate policy, and only 33.7% in government policy. It should be noted that among the answer options there is no such obvious factor that, for substantive reasons, should appear in this type of survey, as "Monetary policy of the central bank". It can be presumed that it happened so because the questioner assumes that in the public perception in the times of the Law and Justice, PiS, ideological and political formation's power, the Polish central bank, formally and statutorily independent of the government, is its de facto arm implementing the government policy.

2022 has been a time of rapidly changing inflation rate forecasts. Its conditions are uniquely unstable, so it is not surprising that if not every month, then every quarter, revised forecasts appear. They are most often characterized by the fact that in the short term, inflation is expected to be higher than assumed in the earlier forecast, while in the two–three-year period, it is expected to fall radically, close to the so-called inflation target set by the central bank. What is important, this type of analysis and forecasting explicitly exposes the decomposition of the inflation rate into three components, namely the so-called core inflation, which excludes from the calculation price increases considered to be independent of monetary policy, namely food price increases and energy price increases, whose indicators are the other two components of the overall inflation rate.

While in the case of Poland in March 2022, the NBP projected the inflation rate in 2022, 2023 and 2024 at 10.8, 9.0 and 4.2%, respectively, in July it forecast its level in the first two of these years to be much higher—14.2 and 12.3 respectively—and in the third year at a similar level, 4.1%.[2] It is to be expected, as is normal in such circumstances, that subsequent forecasts will provide different indicators, sometimes significantly varying ones. Thus, in a report released in mid-July 2022, the NBP calculates that in the first quarter of the year, with an overall inflation rate (measured by the consumer price index, CPI) of 9.7%, core inflation was 6.6%, food inflation 8.7 and energy inflation 21.7%.[3] The latter indicator was strongly affected by natural gas prices. In mid-August, these prices again increased markedly in Europe. The so-called Dutch Front Month Futures rose to EUR 226 per megawatt hour, as much as ten times above the seasonal average. In contrast, the 3.4 percentage points higher inflation assumed for 2022 in the July forecast was explained by the NBP by about half of the higher than previously forecast core inflation, with high food and rising energy prices accounting for 1.0 and 0.7 percentage points, respectively. For 2023, where the inflation rate forecast in July was 3.3 percentage points higher than that announced in March, the relevant indices were 1.9, 0.3 and 1.1 percentage points, respectively.

The overall price index depends on the structure of household expenditure. In particular, when food becomes very expensive, those who spend a relatively higher proportion of their income on food feel the pinch. Let us immediately highlight that it is for this reason that the current inflation is hitting very hard the population of poor countries, where food purchases are a substantial part of the expenditure. In Poland, around 26% of the overall consumer spending is on food (including soft drinks). In the richest countries, it is less than 10%, while in low-income countries, it is on average about half of the household budgets. In the poorest countries, this share can be as high as two-thirds of the total, yet very modest, spending.

The minimum old-age pension in Poland in 2022 was 1,338 zlotys, or ca. USD 300 at the market exchange rate. With such income, with the inflation of a dozen or so percent, the purchasing power of someone already suffering from poverty decreased even more, despite periodic valorization. Because the rate of growth of food prices is above average, it is difficult to make ends meet, and sometimes without family help or social assistance, it is just impossible. In the case of Somalia, in 2022 as much as 80% of the food was imported. And this extremely poor country is tormented not only by inflation but also by drought and terrorism, civil war and the lack of efficient administration. A pastoralist herder before the current drought and high inflation got the equivalent of USD 40 for a goat sold at the market, and he could feed his family of ten for a month. Now, mainly due to the surge in imported grain prices, the income he gets for a skinny goat lasts only for ten days. His family is facing hunger.

Household budget surveys are repeated every few years, but in some countries, they have not been done for a whole decade. The World Bank estimates that in South Asia, food purchases consume around 60% of expenditure. It provides more comparative data for 2010, according to which the share of food expenditure in the poorest countries averaged 53.9%, and in the extreme case, in Mozambique, as much as 63%. According to methodological terms used by the World Bank, half of humanity leaves in the poorest countries in which the daily income per capita did not exceed USD 2.97 in 2010 (calculated at the purchasing power parity). Low incomes between USD 2.97 and USD 8.44 were earned by another 25% of the world's population, medium incomes between USD 8.44 and 23.03 by another 15%, and the remaining 10% earned over USD 23.03.[4]

As a consequence of the various disturbances, there were concerns that not only specific countries but the entire global economy is at risk of stagflation. But it is not so much of a risk that it will come as it is already here if by 'stagflation' we mean the process of a simultaneous slowdown in the rate of economic growth and acceleration in the rate of price increases. It can be observed in most countries. If we stick to the stricter definition of stagflation, i.e. a situation in which literal stagnation, i.e. near-zero growth, and inflation, not necessarily accelerating, coexist, it is still ahead of us. Also ahead of us is a possible slumpflation, i.e. a recession with accompanying inflation. For some countries this is already guaranteed, others may yet avoid this worst combination depending on their vulnerability to external shocks caused by anti-Russian restrictions and Russian retaliation and their own economic policies. But there are also those where both inflation and economic growth rates can rise. Such cases will occur in economies with particularly favorable terms of trade when the prices of goods they export rise faster than those they import. Under current circumstances, this particularly applies to countries exporting energy resources and significant food surpluses.

Yet another view on stagflation is to treat this phenomenon as a simultaneous rise in inflation and unemployment rates. In many countries, this was still unnoticed in the summer of 2022, as unemployment was still not rising, although the rate of production was already falling. Moreover, there were even labor shortages recorded. From California to Kansai, from Bavaria to Piedmont, from Tokyo to Kuala Lumpur, one hears complaints about the lack of hands and minds (more hands) to work. This is partly due to the economic overheating, and partly due to the intentionally temporary withdrawal of some workers from the labor market, but by now to their professional deactivation; some of them do not return to work voluntarily, especially if, in their opinion, it is not sufficiently attractive in terms of earnings. Now unemployment will be rising, perhaps even for the next few years. So, the prices will continue to rise as well, and so it will be classic stagflation, the severity of which can be measured in a simplified manner by the rate of the so-called economic misery index, i.e. the sum of inflation and unemployment rates.

The combination of the two, i.e. inflation and unemployment, fundamentally depends on the economic policy framework applied—the interacting fiscal policy of the government and the monetary policy of the central bank. In practice, it varies, also under the influence of various long-term structural, cultural and political conditions. In large, underdeveloped countries such extremely different situations may occur, as was the case in mid-2022, when Pakistan and South Africa had inflation and unemployment rates of 21.3 and 6.3% in the former and 6.6 and 34.5% in the latter, respectively. Due to the incomplete comparability of the data, caution must be exercised in drawing conclusions, but the dissimilarities in the different approaches to tackling inflation and unemployment in such diverse economies (and political systems) as China and Denmark, where these rates stood at 2.5 and 5.9 and 8.2 and 2.5%, respectively, are striking. In the countries of the Euro area, the situations also varied significantly; in some cases, the two rates were close to each other, such as in Spain, where inflation was 10.2% and unemployment 13.1%, or in Greece, where they were almost equal, at 12.1 and 12.7%, respectively, while in others they were very widely divergent, notably in the Czech Republic, where, according to official figures, the inflation rate reached as high as 17.2%, while the unemployment rate fell to just 2.5%.

If central banks continue to raise interest rates aggressively, relatively lower—compared to a situation of unchanged interest rates—will be inflation rates, but in the wake of slower and slower output growth resulting from more expensive working capital and investment credit, unemployment will become increasingly high. Raising interest rates weakens the housing market and demand for building materials—from wood and glass to cement and copper—and limits consumer credit for cars and household appliances, which in turn reduces the demand for other raw materials such as aluminum. As a result, the entire economy is cooling down, with the obvious consequences for the relatively lower employment level.

The situation is different in China, where inflation in the summer of 2022 was only 2.7% and the economic policy has other serious problems, especially deep imbalances and the debt crisis in the housing market. Therefore, at the end of August, the central bank cut the five-year interest rate to 4.2%, which reduces the cost of paying off mortgage loans, and cut by a minimal margin, just by 0.05 percentage point, from 3.7 to 3.65%, the annual prime rate, which is usually used in determining corporate loans. These moves are expected to bolster the real estate industry, which is in dire straits.

The dilemma of inflation *versus* unemployment is becoming an ever more acute problem for economic policy and is clearly becoming politicized, as is evident in the vast world from the USA to China, from Brazil to Thailand, as the alternative combinations have different effects on the condition of households and businesses, and both have different effects on public moods, which in turn affects people's political preferences, and after all, there are always some new elections to come…

Let us assume for a moment that, although this can be done to a limited extent in practice, fiscal and monetary authorities are able to fully manipulate the components of the economic misery rate, which is, for example, 20% (there was a similar situation in Poland in summer of 2022, when prices were 15–16% higher than a year earlier and the unemployment rate was slightly below 5%). Which option should be chosen? An option with 15% inflation and 5% unemployment? Or perhaps the other way around: 5% inflation and 15% unemployment? How about a median state where both rates are 10%? Which option should be chosen? The question of "which option" means "why this particular option", because the economic, social and political consequences are different when the inflation rate is very high and unemployment is low, and different when there is mass unemployment but inflation is relatively low. So, which option should be chosen?

We may look at this dilemma another way, this time through the prism of an alternative: higher growth rates of production and real incomes at a higher rate of price growth, or slower growth of production and real income at a lower rate of inflation (and hence, less of inflationary income redistribution)? Simply put, we assume that changes in the dynamics of production are closely correlated with changes in the dynamics of real income. Let us also assume that the specific rate of the sacrifice of economic dynamics on the altar of the fight against inflation is 0.25, which means that lowering the inflation rate by one percentage point reduces the GDP growth rate by a quarter of a percentage point; or otherwise, to reduce the growth rate of the general price level by four percentage points we must pay with a loss of one percentage point of GDP growth. What should be chosen? Let us assume that we have inflation of 16%, and GDP grows in real terms (i.e. after eliminating the effects of inflation) by 4%. Should radical measures of monetary policy (interest rate increases) and fiscal policy (tax increases) reduce demand so much that inflation would drop to 12% at the cost of lowering the production growth rate to 3%? What about cutting inflation down to 4% at the cost of slowing down the production dynamics to 1%? Or maybe pick the extreme variant and reset both indicators, when neither prices nor production is rising? What should be chosen?

Someone will say that both rates must be reduced at the same time; both inflation and unemployment should fall. Although some economists used to say this was impossible, referring to the relationship captured in the so-called Phillips curve, which describes the alternative in question, and opposition politicians gave no credence to such a concept, in Poland, for example, they managed to radically reduce both rates between 1993 and 1997: inflation by two-thirds and unemployment by one-third. What is important, at the same time, GDP per capita—in real terms, i.e. after eliminating the effects of inflation—rose by as much as 28%, a record for a four-year period during the past 50 years. Such a scale of change for the better was possible at the time because not only were effective economic policies being pursued that properly defined their objectives and did not confuse them with the means and were based on the correct application of economic theory to practice, but external conditions were also far more favorable. Nonetheless, there is no doubt that also now the policy can be clearly better than it is with its visible results. For this to happen, not only the economy needs to become much more knowledge-based. The policy must also be based on knowledge, especially on the knowledge that, in relation to macro problems, is provided by political economy, which tells us what and why things happen in the interactions between the national economy-society-state-world, and in relation to micro problems, by behavioral economics, which in turn teaches us how and why people in their roles as consumers and producers make decisions.[5]

It is also worth giving some attention to the unexpected emergence of a phenomenon that is not normally seen in market economies, which I have already called shortageflation in the past.[6] This involves the co-existence of a process of rising general price levels and market shortages of goods. Since this phenomenon temporarily occurred in capitalist countries during the Second World War and permanently, albeit with varying intensity, in socialist countries with centrally planned economies, and happened again due to the market disruption caused by the COVID-19 pandemic, I have referred to such a situation as shortageflation 3.0.[7] Should we be talking about shortageflation 4.0 now, when, as a result of the aftermath of the Russian–Ukrainian conflict, despite rising prices, supply shortages are once again occurring and, in many cases, the market cleaning prices mechanism i.e. balancing supply and demand streams—is not working in both production and consumption spheres, being as painful for businesses as for households? Well, I do not think we are going to introduce more neologisms to describe a weird situation where there are four terrible maladies: stagnation, unemployment, inflation and shortages, or recession, unemployment, inflation and shortages. How awkward the terms stag-shortageflation or slump-shortageflation would sound?

Notes

1. United Surveys for "Dziennik Gazeta Prawna" and RMF FM, July 5, 2022.
2. "Projection of inflation and economic growth of the National Bank of Poland based on the NECMOD model", National Bank of Poland, 12 July 2022 (https://www.nbp.pl/polityka_pieniezna/dokumenty/raport_o_inflacji/necmod_lipiec_2022.pdf; access 12.07.2021).
3. Here, the NBP uses imprecise terms of 'food price inflation' and 'energy price inflation'. Inflation is an income-redistributing increase in the general price level. It is therefore inappropriate to speak of 'food price inflation', as this sounds like a 'general increase in the price level of food's price'.
4. "Global Consumption Database: Tables, Charts and Technical Notes", The World Bank (https://datatopics.worldbank.org/consumption/detail; access 18.07.2022).
5. Kahneman, Daniel, "Thinking, fast and slow", Farrar, Strauss and Giroux, New York, 2011.
6. Grzegorz W. Kolodko, Walter W. McMahon, "Stagflation and Shortageflation: A Comparative Approach", "Kyklos", 1987, Vol. 40, No. 2, pp. 176–197.
7. Grzegorz W. Kolodko, "Shortageflation 3.0: War Economy—State Socialism—Pandemic Crisis", "Acta Oeconomica", 2021, Special Issue, pp. 13–34.

11

A Very Expensive War is Getting Even More Expensive

In deciding to attack Ukraine, the Russian President, being aware of his prestige and power, certainly expected to be understood and, moreover, supported by the majority of the population. Before the aggression, we could read that "After twenty years as president or prime minister, Vladimir Putin remains the powerful and popular leader of his nation, perhaps more than any other Russian leader since the revolution of 1917. His new authoritarianism is perceived—not only in his own country—as the most successful Russian regime in generations. (…) As such, it serves as a model for new authoritarians in other countries."[1] Again, the question arises: in the wake of the war with Ukraine, will this model fade or become even more glaring? The answer does not have to be straightforward, because while some countries may want to emulate Russia, others at the same time will stay away from it as much as possible. It is enough to compare its neighbors such as the former Soviet republics of Lithuania and Belarus or Turkmenistan and Uzbekistan.

A very expensive war is getting even more expensive. The war—even without sanctions—is very costly for Russia and each day is becoming more costly. Against this background, it is speculated that "If Russia starts to lose ground on the battlefield, dissent and infighting may spread in the Kremlin. (…) The West can raise the cost to Russia of a long war by continuing to press sanctions, which threaten lasting harm to Russia's economy. It can split Russia's elites from Mr. Putin by welcoming dissenters from business and politics, and encouraging them to see that their country should not throw away its future on a pointless and costly campaign."[2] This can be hoped for, but how long will it take for such a path of change to become a reality? Is it not too long and too costly for the unfortunate Ukrainians on the one hand, and for the people living away from the frontline who suffer the consequences of the ricochets of restrictions on the other? Is it really worth it?

Political calculations made in various capitals quite differently estimate and weigh the costs—and the benefits, because there is plenty of these for some either—of dragging out the war. Let me quote, referring to another conflict and the sanctions involved, the very telling opinion of Madeleine Albright, former US Secretary of State, expressed during a television interview on CBS's "60 min". When, following the imposition of US sanctions on Iraq after the 1991 Gulf War, she was asked (she was then US ambassador to the UN) that as a consequence: "half a million Iraqi children died (…) Was such a price worth it?", she replied: "I think that is a very hard choice, but the price is worth it".[3] Others think differently.

It was absolutely not worth it, just as it is not worth it now to contribute with sanctions and retaliation to them to the prolongation of the Ukrainian crisis, given not only the local tragedies but also its side effects elsewhere, including the possibility of humanitarian crises far away. The further away it is, the less it hurts, but even if this is how the psychological and political mechanisms work, that nearby a thousand deaths is like more than a million in remote countries in sub-Saharan Africa, the Middle East or South Asia, one must also be aware of the further consequences of such a state of affairs. Humanitarian crises and accompanying social and political unrest in distant countries indirectly affected by the Russia–Ukraine hot clash and the Russia–West cold war will intensify waves of emigration. Refugees will number in the tens of millions. There will be more and more of them—especially those arriving in Europe—and yet the countries they reach are not able to cope with it already. In May 2022—three months after Russia's invasion of Ukraine, from which an estimated 5 million people escaped at the time—the number of people forced to flee conflicts, violence, human rights violations and persecution worldwide exceeded 100 million.[4]

According to the United Nations High Commissioner for Refugees, UNHCR, data, from the beginning of the war until the end of May, 6,890,245 people had crossed the border to leave Ukraine, but at the same time, 2,125,235 people had returned to it. Thus, 4,765,010 people stayed abroad. These numbers changed significantly over the next two months. By the end of July, the number of people, who left Ukraine, increased to 10,290,039, and those who returned to 4,230,116. Thus, as many as 6,059,923 more Ukrainians remained abroad than before the Russian invasion; this quantity is constantly changing. If all of them were treated as

11 A Very Expensive War is Getting Even More Expensive

refugees, their number would be almost the same as the number of refugees from Syria, and in relative terms—in relation to the country's population—it would be the second most dramatic case in the world, after Syria. However, in these two months—in June and July 2022—most of the people crossing the Ukrainian border, mainly with Poland, were not refugees from the horrors of war, but rather regular non-war economic emigration. Mainly, similar to previous years, they were people working or looking for a job in Poland and in Western European countries. So it has been in the subsequent months.

One should not forget the already occurring catastrophic humanitarian situations on so much more painful scale than the one in Ukraine. The UN estimates that, in total, around 750 million people worldwide (that is more than the population of Europe or 200 million more than the population of North and Central America combined) require urgent assistance because they are not able to cope on their own with the ills of security, disease, malnutrition and hunger as well as natural disasters that afflict them.

Far worse than in Ukraine is the situation of the population in Afghanistan, Bangladesh, Chad, Ethiopia, part of Myanmar, Syria and Yemen where 377,000 people have died as a result of fighting, famine and disease, three-quarters of the population can only survive with meager foreign aid, and only half of the hospitals and clinics there are somehow functioning.[5] The food consumed there is 90 percent imported and, in the summer of 2022, it was 120 percent more expensive than the year before. A staggering half a million people have died in Ethiopian Tigray province during the year and a half of armed conflict there. It is estimated that 50,000 to 100,000 died in the fighting, 150,000 to 200,000 died of starvation and more than 100,000 as a result of lack of health care.[6] In Chad, where the median age is only 16, there are six doctors per 100,000 people. It is mainly the lack of appropriate medical care that contributes to the horror that out of 100,000 live births, as many as 6,548 infants die, and 1,140 mothers pass away in childbirth. For comparison, in Poland, these numbers are 416 and 2, respectively.

These appalling tragedies are no consolation to Ukraine, nor do they diminish the scale of the Ukrainian tragedy, but unfortunately the Director General of the World Health Organization, WHO, Tedros Adhanom Ghebreyesus, is right when he says that people of different races are not treated equally and doubts if "…the world really gives equal attention to black and white lives."[7] As befits the head of an international organization spanning the globe, he stresses that while humanitarian aid to Ukraine is very important, others must not be neglected. Worse still, some countries providing help are far more eager to provide military aid—and this is often no aid at all, but on the contrary, it is harmful—rather than humanitarian aid.

Much depends on the political objectives that really guide the parties engaging in the conflict. If we assume for a moment that, with regard to the Russian–Ukrainian clash, the actual objectives coincide with those officially proclaimed—yet so often this is not the case—then much also depends on the assumptions that are made in formulating assessments and constructing strategies of action. Someone may share the view that "You can see where Mr. Putin is heading. He will take as much of Ukraine as he can, declare victory and then call on Western nations to impose his terms on Ukraine. In exchange, he will spare the rest of the world from ruin, hunger, cold and the threat of nuclear Armageddon. To accept that deal would be a grave miscalculation. Ukraine would face permanent Russian aggression. The more Mr. Putin believes he has succeeded in Ukraine, the more belligerent he will become. He set out his ambitions in a speech this month [July 2022], smirking as he talked about how Peter the Great seized parts of Sweden. He will fight tomorrow with whatever weapons work for him today. That means resorting to war crimes and nuclear threats, starving the world and freezing Europe."[8] If this is how someone sees things, then it can be understood why one advocates prolonging the war as potentially the only way to win it if it could not be nipped in the bud. But someone else may disagree with the quoted opinion, and then they may be right that the war needs to be ended as soon as possible—even at the cost of Ukraine losing some of its territories—in order to be able to deal peacefully with solving problems, of which there is plenty.

Notes

1. Jerzy J. Wiatr, *op. cit.*, p. 162.
2. "How to win…", *op. cit.*
3. Jon Jackson, "Madeleine Albright Saying Iraqi Kids' Deaths 'Worth It' Resurfaces", "Newsweek", March 25, 2022 (https://www.newsweek.com/watch-madeleine-albright-saying-iraqi-kids-deaths-worth-it-resurfaces-1691193; access 3.07.2022).
4. "Ukraine, other conflicts push forcibly displaced total over 100 million for first time", The United Nations High Commissioner for Refugees, UNHCR, 23 May, 2022 (https://www.unhcr.org/en-us/news/press/2022/5/628a389e4/unhcr-ukraine-other-conflicts-push-forcibly-displaced-total-100-million.html; access 11.07.2022).

5. "War-ravaged Yemen gets a truce and dumps a tired president", "The Economist", April 16, 2022 (https://www.economist.com/middle-east-and-africa/2022/04/16/war-ravaged-yemen-gets-a-truce-and-dumps-a-tired-president; access 16.04.2022).
6. Geoffrey York, "Tigray war has seen up to half a million dead from violence and starvation, say researchers", "The Globe and Mail", March 15, 2022 (https://www.theglobeandmail.com/world/article-tigray-war-has-seen-up-to-half-a-million-dead-from-violence-and/); access 20.03.2022). See also "We Will Erase You from This Land: Crimes Against Humanity and Ethnic Cleansing in Ethiopia's Western Tigray Zone", Human Rights Watch and Amnesty International, April 2022 (https://www.hrw.org/report/2022/04/06/we-will-erase-you-land/crimes-against-humanity-and-ethnic-cleansing-ethiopias; access 10.07.2022).
7. "Ukraine attention shows bias against black lives, WHO chief says", "BBC News", April 13, 2022 (https://www.bbc.com/news/world-61101732; access 20.04.2022).
8. "How to win Ukraine's long war", "The Economist", June 30, 2022 (https://www.economist.com/leaders/2022/06/30/how-to-win-ukraines-long-war; access 2.07.2022).

12

Globalization Has Taken a Few Powerful Blows But Has not Been Knocked Out

While in the course of the previous three decades the word "globalization" became the keyword for opening the discussions on almost all economic problems, during the last three years—in the context of the anti-globalization policies of the previous (and let's hope not future!) US President Donald Trump, the resurgence of protectionist practices, Cold War resentments in politics and successive waves of the coronavirus pandemic—the prevailing view has been that globalization is over, or at least that its future trends have been reversed. To the surprise of many commentators, President Biden's policies are also contributing to these trends, as he is essentially continuing the courses of action taken by his predecessor. One of his main policy objectives is to slow down the expansion of the Chinese economy and to try to halt its relentless march to an increasingly powerful position in the world.

This, among other things, is to be served by a project with the nice name of the Indo-Pacific Economic Framework for Prosperity, IPEF,[1] launched at the initiative of the American President in May 2022. However, the IPEF is essentially to be limited to discussing a variety of otherwise non-trivial topics—from decarbonization to data sharing—but nothing is said there about reducing trade barriers. This is to be negotiated within the framework of another regional structure, the Trans-Pacific Partnership, TPP,[2] from which President Trump withdrew the US shortly after its formation in 2016. Now, they are in the IPEF, they are not in the TPP, although a cross-party group in Washington has become active lobbying for the return of the US to the TPP. Seven countries are members of both the IPEF and TPP groupings, namely Australia, Brunei, Japan, Malaysia, New Zealand Singapore and Vietnam. There is no China in any of these because one of the tasks of these regional formations is to weaken China's position and, above all, to reduce the degree of dependence on the Chinese link in the supply and production chains.

What is important is that some countries act "on two fronts" —the American-led anti-Chinese one—and hence the IPEF – but at the same time the more pluralistic one that China is part of, namely the Regional Comprehensive Economic Partnership, ECEP, created in 2021. Ten members of the Association of Southeast Asian States, ASEAN, namely Brunei, Cambodia, Indonesia, Laos, Malaysia, Myanmar, the Philippines, Singapore, Thailand and Vietnam are participating in this integration grouping as well as Australia, Japan, South Korea and New Zealand, allies to the US.

All of this has important implications for the reconfiguration of world trade, which after all is one of the strongest drivers of globalization. According to Refinitiv Datastream calculations, from the US administration's imposition of anti-China trade sanctions in mid-2018 to April 2022, the share of China's imports to the US in its total imports of foreign goods has fallen by nearly five percentage points, from just under 22 percent to just over 17 percent. Over the same period, the shape of the curve showing the rise in the share of imports from ASEAN economies is almost a mirror image of the falling Chinese curve; the share of imports from the region in total US imports rose by almost 4 percentage points, from 7 to over 10 percent. Tariffs on the import of Chinese products, introduced as part of the trade war declared against China by the Trump administration, have risen from around 3 percent to almost 20 percent during this quadrennium. Naturally, China responded to such a dictum by raising its import tariffs on US products, this time from around 7.5 to over 21 percent. As a result of this unfortunate trade war, almost 65 percent of Chinese exports to the US and around 57 percent of US exports to China are subject to protectionist barriers.

Anti-import tariffs targeting Chinese exports are essentially being maintained by the Biden administration. This is paid for by US consumers, to whom the imported goods go indirectly, and most often directly in the form of final consumer goods. Even if the White House is considering a reduction in tariffs in order to alleviate some of the inflationary pressures that such protectionist practices exacerbate, it is again not common-sense economic arguments that are decisive, but political motives, rather lacking such a sense in recent times. The ruling Democrats fear that such moves would be perceived by the opposing Republicans as a sign of subservience to China, something that Republicans are ruthlessly exploiting in the campaign leading up to the November 2022 congressional elections, and both believe that this is how the Chinese themselves might interpret it. Therefore, a moderate adjustment of the applied tariff and non-tariff sanctions can be expected at most. Import duties on shoes will probably fall, which people will notice immediately in the shops, but they will rise on microchips, which they will feel later, after the elections.

This is how this anti-China trade war has by no means eliminated the trade deficit on the US side, as President Trump dreamt of, but has only changed the geographical structure of the trade. Sources of the structural imbalance with regard to imports and exports lie in the inadequate competitiveness of the American economy, and not in the fact that others—not only the Chinese but also the Mexicans and even political allies from Canada, the European Union, Japan and South Korea—in the opinion of not only Trump, for there are many economic ignoramuses, are cheating the poor Americans.

Some authors see signs of retreat from globalization and move toward regionalization not only in these attempts to create regional structures—and there are, after all, more of them on all continents. I, on the other hand, believe—that regionalisms are not so much a denial or an obstacle to the continuation of globalization as they can be a lever for its advancement. Now, instead of integrating starting from pieces of more than two hundred states and dependent territories, coordinated and deepened economic cooperation and trade can—as it already does—take place between entire groupings, for example between the European Union and Mercosur[3] in South America or between SADC[4] in southern and ECOWAS[5] in western Africa.

The view that globalization is in decline is becoming quite widespread both among the general public and among some professional economists. I think they are wrong. Globalization has taken a few powerful blows but has not been knocked out. A shop assistant in a village near Warsaw is right: when I pointed out that she sells fruit from as many as 14 countries, from China (plums) to Brazil (melons), from South Africa (pears) to Ecuador (pineapples), from Turkey (grapes) to Morocco (mandarins), she succinctly commented: globalization. Those economists who draw attention to the persistence of the fundamental positive features of globalization, especially the economies of scale (lowering of unit costs due to increased scope of production linked to the sales in foreign markets), the importance of supply chains for efficiency, and the possibility of more profitable capital investment and direct investment, are right. Those who say that the war in Ukraine and its international consequences are finishing off the already fragile globalization are wrong.

Let us once again recall the definition of globalization. It is a historical and spontaneous process of liberalization and integration of national economies, previously functioning to a certain extent separately, markets for commodities, internationally tradeable services and capital, as well as labor (although with delays and constraints due to cultural and political considerations)—into one interdependent, internally coupled global system. What happens here depends on what happens elsewhere and causes something else to happen yet somewhere else. By its very nature, this is an irreversible process in this phase of civilization. Again having accepted certain conjunctures, and especially assuming that a total world war would not occur. And that is what I consistently assume; it will not occur.

There is, however, a widespread view that the shock of Russian aggression—and more specifically its geopolitical and transnational economic consequences—is breaking the bonds that are the essence of globalization: free trade, capital flows, technology transfer, coordination of regulations relating to the international and global scale of economic exchange. Not at all. Globalization is a vital process. While some ties are broken, others are born, as some weaken, others are strengthened. World trading volumes in relation to world production have indeed fallen from around 60 percent in 2010 to around 52 percent in 2020—and are likely to continue to fall for several more years—but it is also true that in 2022, they were larger than at any time in history before 2003. Moreover, we should add that the essence of globalization is not to increase trading volumes continuously every decade, and certainly not every year, but for them to be large enough so that the various points on the economic map of the world are effectively and pro-developmentally interlinked. And so it is.

We should therefore speak not of a breakdown of globalization, but of its restructuring. It does not need to be reinvented, as "The Economist" suggests,[6] but its mechanisms certainly need to be considerably modified. In particular, the imperative to re-institutionalize globalization in terms of making it more inclusive remains fully valid, which is nothing new. The World Bank has been talking about this for twenty years, and China has been increasingly vocal over the past few years in describing such desirable globalization as a win–win—beneficial for all involved parties. What is new, on the other hand, is that sanctions punishing Russia for its behavior are an attempt to cut it off as much as possible from the global economic circuit. But what, realistically speaking, might be the extent of it?

On the one hand, from the point of view of Russia itself, it has already been isolated from the world economy to a considerable degree, and thus partly excluded from participation in globalization, which it has otherwise not been able to benefit from in the past as much as other countries, including its neighbors such as little Estonia, medium-sized Poland, big Japan or large China. From the world's point of view, on the other hand, the isolation of Russia—while by no means to be underestimated—does not cause a mortal wound to the globalized economy. It certainly harms it above all where it is difficult, costly and time-consuming to change Russian raw material supplies to alternative sources, and does not serve those who need to find other markets for their goods. The rest of the world can cope much easier without deeper involvement in Russia's economy, which produced only 3.1 percent of global output in 2021, calculated according to the purchasing power parity, or 1,9 percent in current USD, than Russia can cope with drastically reduced access to the rest of the world.

However, a fracture is emerging in the global economic system shaped by thirty-plus years of the contemporary phase of globalization, which is damaging but not destroying it, because it is temporary. In the medium term, adjustment processes are taking place in various companies in Russia-sanctioning countries and in the entire national economies of the countries that are loosening or outright eliminating economic exchange with Russia. At the same time, other economies of the numerous countries that have not joined the anti-Russian sanctions, and the companies operating there, will seize the opportunities that come their way to deepen their economic relations with Russia wherever it is profitable for them to do so. As a result, in the wake of Western restrictions, the scale of the Russian economy's coupling with a great part of the world—the less developed countries such as China, India, Brazil, South Africa, Indonesia, Pakistan, Egypt—may be even greater than before. Another perverse effect?

In the long term, the economies of the West will return to Russia—for its raw materials, for its markets, for the profits from the possibility to invest capital profitably, for working with its professionals. This time, too, we do not know what the long term means, but it will not be centuries; decades will suffice. Also long? Long, but time is flying fast. Globalization therefore continues, and although it has again twisted its face a little, this is not a perpetual blemish but a temporary grimace.

Notes

1. Fourteen countries belong to the IPEF: Australia, Brunei, Fiji, India, Indonesia, Japan, Malaysia, New Zealand, the Philippines, Singapore, South Korea, Thailand, the United States and Vietnam.

2. TPP member states are: Australia, Brunei, Chile, Japan, Malaysia, Mexico, New Zealand, Peru, Singapore and Vietnam.
3. The members of Mercosur (Spanish: Mercado Común del Sur), Common Market of the South are: Argentina, Brazil, Paraguay, Uruguay and Venezuela, which has been suspended from membership since 2016 under regional sanctions.
4. The SADC group, the Southern African Development Community, includes Angola, Botswana, Democratic Republic of the Congo, Eswatini, Lesotho, Madagascar, Malawi, Mauritius, Mozambique, Namibia, Seychelles, South Africa, Tanzania, Zambia and Zimbabwe.
5. ECOWAS, Economic Community of West African States, consists of Benin, Burkina Faso, Cape Verde, Côte d'Ivoire, the Gambia, Ghana, Guinea, Guinea-Bissau, Liberia, Mali, Niger, Nigeria, Senegal, Sierra Leone and Togo.
6. "Reinventing globalisation", "The Economist", June 18, 2022 (https://www.economist.com/weeklyedition/2022-06-18; access 18.06.2022).

13

Help Ukraine to Rise from the Ruins

The most tragic dimension of Russia's invasion of Ukraine is the thousands of casualties, including civilians, and the humanitarian crisis accompanying this senseless war, but the material losses are also enormous. While before the invasion the International Monetary Fund projected an increase in Ukraine's GDP of 3.6% for 2022, in the first month of the war, the Economist Intelligence Unit assumed that it would fall by 46.5% in real terms; instead of rising to an already modest 204 billion in current international dollars, it fell to a measly 97 billion—as much as Ethiopia or Ecuador, less than one-sixth in Poland. Such a catastrophic recession deprives the public finance system of revenues estimated by the Ukrainian authorities at around USD 5 billion a month, implying a budget deficit in 2022 of about 25% of GDP. A year earlier, it was 3.5%. The lack of funds in the state coffers, and even more so rickety production and service activity bringing employees low wages and high unemployment led to a dramatic increase in the percentage of people living below the poverty line. According to April estimates of the United Nations Development Program, UNDP, in the event of a recession of only 20%, the share of people with a daily income below USD 5.50 would be 9%, and if GDP fell by as much as 60%, that would be 28%.[1] In the year preceding the war, it was only 2.5%. The longer the armed conflict lasts, the more poverty. A few months later, the World Bank pessimistically calculated the possibility of increasing the population living in poverty at the end of 2023 to 55%, which, however, seems to be an exaggerated estimate. In the Ukrainian reality, this would mean that more than half of the population

© The Author(s), under exclusive license to Springer Nature Switzerland AG 2023
G. W. Kolodko, *Global Consequences of Russia's Invasion of Ukraine*, https://doi.org/10.1007/978-3-031-24263-2_13

has to make ends meet on less than 51 hryvnias a day, given that the dollar exchange rate in line with purchasing power is estimated at 9.28 hryvnias. But let's not forget that 30% of inhabitants are rural population, a large part of which support their standard of living by consuming food from the natural farming economy, whose products do not pass the market and their total value may not be taken fully into account in consumption estimates. For comparison, in Poland, the same measure implies a daily income of 10.12 zlotys, i.e. about 310 zlotys per month.[2] There are no such cases anymore, but situations of severe poverty may very rarely occur, when after settling all obligatory bills and payments, someone is left with no more than 10 zlotys a day for all remaining expenses.

According to Ukrainian Prime Minister Denys Shmyhal, taking into account both the damage already done and the damage to production that will be incurred in the years to come as a result of the war, the losses exceed one trillion dollars, of which the devastation of infrastructure is 120 billion. After just over four months of clashes, he stated at a conference on the prospects for rebuilding war-devastated Ukraine that the cost would be USD 750 billion. This meeting, held on 4 July 2022 in the Swiss city of Lugano, was attended by more than 40 countries and representatives of important international organizations, including the European Investment Bank, EIB, and the Organization for Economic Cooperation and Development, OECD.

In October, at another international conference, more modest, but still quite significant amounts were discussed. The German Marshall Fund, GMF, in a report prepared for the occasion, talks about USD 100 billion spread over many years. There is a reason why Berlin was chosen as the venue for the conference, thus emphasizing that it is Germany, as Europe's largest economy and also a member of the G7, that will play a particularly significant role in the post-war reconstruction of Ukraine. It is impossible not to notice what a dissonance in the process of preparing for the financing of this aid are the unfortunate Poland's claims for over 60 times larger amount of compensation for war damage of quite distant times. It is worth realizing that, although arising from very different circumstances, both a part of Ukraine's expectations and all the Polish government's demands toward Germany are addressed to the same place: the German budget and German taxpayers. If someone asks them to which of these alternative destinations they would possibly be willing to pay higher taxes for a few or several years, the answer should not come as a surprise: Ukraine. This is not just because Poland has long since recovered from the post-war ruins and is several times richer than its eastern neighbor and Ukraine is still to be rebuilt after a completely different war.

Even if these estimates turn out to be exaggerated, the losses in Ukraine are indeed enormous. Other calculations are emerging, and there will be more of them, ranging from USD 100 billion to a trillion dollars, and perhaps even more. In fact, they will never be measured precisely. These will always be more or less strict estimates based on various assumptions about actual initial and drawn-out, direct and indirect, primary and secondary, *stricte* financial and economic sensu *largo* costs.

Apart from intangible losses, the costs of this nightmarish conflict can be classified and grouped in various ways. I think it might be useful to put them into a long dozen categories:

1. Labor productivity losses caused by social stress and psychological trauma.
2. Failures in production and services resulting from disturbances in the functioning of supply chains.
3. Damage and failures in transport that affect all sectors of the economy.
4. Losses in services, industry and agriculture caused by the shortage of manpower resulted from the conscription of men to the army and internal and foreign migration of the masses of the population.
5. Industrial losses due to the destruction of enterprises in the area of armed conflicts and the loss of effective control over undamaged enterprises.
6. Losses in agriculture caused by the shrinkage of arable soils and the decline in the number of field workers due to hastened emigration to Western Europe.
7. Losses in the energy sector caused by devastated infrastructure and declining fuel supply.
8. Losses in non-produced manufacture and non-rendered services due to the administrative shift of material supplies and other resources from the civil to the military sector.
9. Export losses due to blockades of Black Sea ports.
10. Losses accrued from the dearth of bank credit for the private sector and budget financing for the public sector.
11. Perturbations resulting from the deficit of hard convertible currencies and the volatility of the hryvnia exchange rate.
12. Losses caused by distortions in the capital market and inflation.
13. Losses caused by the freezing and abandonment of foreign direct investment.

The losses will be lower, the sooner the war ends, which must be sought in every possible way, and the lower the losses, the more it is possible to mitigate the long-term economic effects of the war. In the current phase of the crisis, humanitarian and military aid to Ukraine defending itself is most urgent. The day will come, however, when the gunshots and explosions will fall silent. At that point, it will no longer be just short-term assistance that will be important, but above all long-term support.

Undeniably, when Prime Minister Shmyhal talks about rebuilding Ukraine from the devastation, he is thinking of the whole of his country, without compromising any territory, including the Donbas, which was most devastated by the fighting, and the southern part of the country linking this region with Crimea, annexed in 2014 without any material damage. If, instead, it was to turn out that Russia would occupy the Donbas and annex it once the fighting is over then the cost of rebuilding a truncated Ukraine would be substantially lower. Even if someone in Kyiv counts this way, they do not announce it publicly because of their principled attitude to the treatment of the integrity of Ukrainian lands. It is indisputable, though, that of this USD 750 billion, the lion's share would be taken up by the reconstruction of the Donbas. If it holds on to Ukraine, it will be a worry for Ukraine and those who want to help it. If not, it will be Russia's concern. Whoever rebuilds Mariupol will pay for it. Either way, the reconstruction needs will be enormous and therefore Ukraine cannot be left alone.

Various methods can be used to help Ukraine to rise from the ruins. Particularly important would be the creation of a special financial vehicle of the European Union, to which Ukraine aspires to be a member. It should in time be admitted to the Union, but not in any extraordinary way, by any express route, but once the institutional conditions for integration have been met, as is expected of other countries that already have candidate statuses. In the case of Ukraine, the deoligarchization of the economy is essential. Largely corrupt economic and political structures have hampered the country's development over the years.

According to Economist Intelligence Unit assessments, Ukraine is a hybrid democracy that ranks 87th in comparisons of political systems, between Mexico and Senegal, with a low score of 5.57 (on a scale of 0–10). By contrast, in the Transparency International's compiled ranking of corruption perception, it is placed between Zambia and Niger, and with an index of 32 (on a scale of 0–100) ranks a distant 122nd, not much better than Russia, which is 136th. It was the corruption and inefficient mechanisms of limited democracy which caused that Ukraine's GDP per capita in 2021, counting according to the purchasing power parity, was only 74% of its 1989 level (2017 constant prices), when it was still the second largest republic of the USSR. For comparison, in Poland, this index is 264%.

Now, to support Ukraine's reconstruction from the devastation of war, the European Union should create a special, multi-year financial fund—let's call it a European Fund for Reconstruction of Ukraine, EFRU—whose successive multi-billion-dollar tranches will finance infrastructure investments and co-finance investments in human capital. At the same time, by educating hundreds of thousands of Ukrainian refugees in the various places they fled to, efforts will have to be made to ensure that as many of them as possible wish to return to their homeland in the time of need. Otherwise, what is currently an admirable expression of solidarity and invaluable humanitarian aid will in time turn out to be a de facto brain drain. A bad war should not be a good opportunity to exploit cheap labor and solve one's labor shortage problems at the expense of Ukraine.[3]

Launching such a fund, to which the European Commission should invite the UK, Norway and Switzerland, will not be easy. This costs money and will quickly prove more expensive than supplying weapons. It has only just been possible to organize funding within the EU to combat the COVID-19 coronavirus pandemic, which implies costs running into hundreds of billions of euros. A great deal of it has to be borrowed on financial markets, as the Union does not have sufficient funds for this purpose within its modest budget. This is compounded by the non-transferable energy transition expenditure required to be borne. The European Union, any of its member states, must not turn its back on the agreements made in 2021 at the COP26 summit in Glasgow to combat global warming. Even in such an extraordinary situation as the war in the eastern areas of the continent, it must not be forgotten for a moment that it is climate change that is the greatest challenge facing not only Europeans but humanity as a whole.

Perhaps fraternal funding of Ukraine's post-war reconstruction will require a special solidarity tax, just as Germany did when uniting after the previous Cold War ended three decades ago. Probably that is exactly what it should be, although, for the time being, no one is very willing to announce such a plan. It is a well-known fact that it is always easier to support someone with words than with real money from one's pocket. It is impossible to get the money out of there without additional tax revenues. In turn, the temptation to finance the piling up of expenditure with an inflation tax leads astray, as many countries have already experienced.

A second, unorthodox instrument to help Ukraine's post-war reconstruction should be a fundamental reduction of its foreign debt. How much of an impact this can have, I know from personal experience. In September 1994, after tedious negotiations and an earlier halving of the debt to the state creditors grouped in the Paris Club, I signed an agreement on behalf of Poland, as its Deputy Prime Minister and Minister of Finance, to reduce the Polish debt, also by half, to the private banks organized in the London Club. The considerable amount of reduced debt, USD 6.3 billion, equated to 5.7% of GDP at the time. This gave us not only a breath in the sphere of public finances but above all access to European and global capital markets, which was skillfully taken advantage of by implementing subsequent development policies.

Ukraine's total public debt at the end of 2021 was approximately USD 98 billion, representing 61.7% of GDP.[4] Of this amount, foreign debt was around USD 57 billion (around 36% of GDP). It would be possible for the West, which is so firmly—and rightly—on the side of Ukraine, to substantially reduce these obligations or even cancel them altogether. Such an intention should now be publicly declared, linking the stages of reduction to the progress in deoligarchization and the building of social market economy institutions in place of corrupt state capitalism. The European Union is far more interested in this than the United States, which makes no secret of the fact that it is primarily interested in arms supplies. It should be the EU that takes an unequivocal initiative on this issue and then monitors and oversees the debt relief process. In the opposite direction it is further increasing Ukraine's indebtedness, as was the case of the credits of nearly USD 2 billion granted by the International Monetary Fund and the World Bank immediately in February, and the September loan of EUR 5 billion from the EU, even if these are at interest rates slightly below commercial market rates. Yet even worse is the supply of armaments not free of charge but on credit.

A decade ago, China did not invite Ukraine to join the Central and Eastern European offshoot of its huge, almost global infrastructure project, the Belt and Road Initiative, BRI, commonly known as the New Silk Road.[5] This was probably for geopolitical reasons, as Beijing felt there was no need to irritate Moscow, which considered its large south-eastern neighbor to be a sphere of Russian influence. Although all this has not much economic sense, that is how it could have been. And yet it is enough to look at a map to see that Ukraine lies in a sensitive part of the program area which was first 16 + 1—from Estonia and Latvia in the north to Montenegro and Albania in the south—then, with the addition of Greece in 2019, 17 + 1 and now, with the withdrawal from this initiative by Lithuania in 2021, and Estonia and Latvia in 2022, 14 + 1.[6]

As soon as the ceasefire is declared and the battle dust begins to settle, President Xi Jinping should call President Volodymyr Zelensky and invite Ukraine to join the 14 + 1 and declare his readiness to provide specific assistance to rebuild the devastated economy. Such an act should be perceived neither as anti-Russian nor anti-EU nor as a sign of Chinese expansionism—although some believe that this is exactly how the Americans would treat it, dissuading Kyiv from cooperating with Beijing with the threat of withdrawing military aid—but as China's willingness to join the process of solving the Ukrainian problem. Obviously, also with benefits for the Chinese economy. Along the way, this could revive the somewhat sluggish course of affairs within the BRI in Central and Eastern Europe.

China has significant excess capacities in the construction investment sector (which was otherwise one of the factors behind the launch of the BRI) and is looking to make judicious use of it abroad.[7] In doing so, they have a wealth of experience like few others in infrastructure investments—in the construction of roads, bridges and tunnels, ports, airports and stations, railways, power tractions and internet networks. Quick to learn, Chinese companies have shown that they can adapt these experiences and their technologies to the most diverse conditions—from their own vast country through South Asia and the Middle East to Africa. They have also built a thing or two in Europe, not just in Central and Eastern Europe.

Such a unique triptych—the European Fund for Reconstruction of Ukraine, the cancellation of foreign debt and the invitation of Ukraine to join the 14 + 1 initiative—would be a great economic help to the country that is suffering such misfortune. As soon as the political conditions to do so arise, Ukraine must be earnestly helped, as it will not make it on its own.

Notes

1. "The Development Impact of the War in Ukraine. Initial Projections", United Nations Development Program, New York, April 2022. According to the World Bank's methodology, the purchasing power parity level of USD 5.50 (in 2011 international prices) is a poverty indicator for upper-middle-income countries. Currently about half of the world's population lives below this level.
2. According to the purchasing power parity, the American dollar is equal to 1.84 Polish zlotys or, from the opposite perspective, the zloty can buy as much in Poland as 54 cents in the USA "OECD Data. Purchasing power parities (PPP)", Organization for Economic Cooperation and Development", Paris (https://data.oecd.org/conversion/purchasing-power-parities-ppp.htm#indicator-chart; access 9.08.2022). In Ukraine, the hryvnia can buy as much as one can get for a dime in the USA. See: "PPP conversion factor, GDP (LCU, per international $)"; World Development Indicators, World Bank, Washington, DC, 2022.
3. In the spring of 2022, around 30% of Ukrainians staying in Poland expressed a desire to stay longer. In August, more than half felt like this. Already nearly

750,000 Ukrainians are registered with the Social Insurance Institution, ZUS, and work in Poland legally. According to a survey by employment agency EWL, one in seven visitors from the east would like to stay in Poland for a few years after the end of the war, and 6% would like to stay for good. Only 22% are thinking of returning to their home country as soon as possible.
4. It is now over 100%.
5. Bruno Maçães, "Belt and Road: A Chinese World Order", Hurts, London, 2020.
6. Lithuania left the 17 + 1 format after tightening relations with China following the opening of a Taiwanese trade representative in Vilnius, not under the Taipei brand, but Taiwan. Estonia and Latvia, in turn, have withdrawn from the 16 + 1 in August 2022, no coincidence shortly after Nancy Pelosi's visit in Taipei and US Secretary of Defense Lloyd Austin in Riga. The decisions of all three Baltic states were preceded by Taiwan's lively economic activity in the region and plans of further investments, especially in the field of advanced technologies. So much as for the facts. And now the language of diplomacy. The Latvian Ministry of Foreign Affairs, communicating decision to leave the 16 + 1 format, stated (Estonia's Foreign Ministry spoke in a similar language) that it was doing so "in view of the current priorities of Latvian foreign and trade policy" and that "Latvia will continue to strive for constructive and pragmatic relations with China both bilaterally, as well as through EU-China cooperation based on mutual benefit, respect for international law, human rights and the international rules-based order." As cited in "Latvia's decision to leave cooperation framework of Central and Eastern European Countries and China not to change much", "The Baltic Times", August 12, 2022 (https://www.baltictimes.com/latvia_s_decision_to_l eave_cooperation_framework_of_central_and_eastern_european_countries_ and_china_not_to_change_much_-_expert/; access 19.08.2022).
7. Bruno Maçães, "Belt and Road: A Chinese World Order", Hurts, London, 2020.

14

The Second Cold War is a World War

So, what this is all about, what is happening in our world that got itself into a trap? There is a saying that if we do not know what the deal is, then the deal is money. To some, it undoubtedly is, but the issue is more complicated. The games are played at different levels. At the lowest ones, they are often about one's safety, survival, and a roof over the heads. At the highest ones, for prestige, power and domination. While some are struggling to make ends meet, others struggle for multi-billion dollar profits. Some people just want to live with dignity, others just want to rule. I remember over a quarter of a century ago, being the Deputy Prime Minister and Minister of Finance, that I pouted when I heard from Zbigniew Brzezinski that politics is a game of influence. How so?! After all, policies are about solving economic and social problems pro publico bono. Well, both, but—unfortunately probably more rightful was a political scientist and advisor, not an economist and economic policymaker.

The deal is certainly not about what is officially proclaimed by politicians and media in the countries involved in the Ukrainian crisis in various ways. In fact, only what Ukrainians say when they claim to be fighting for sovereignty and defending the territorial integrity of their homeland, which has been unexpectedly and brutally attacked by a larger and stronger neighbor, can be uncritically accepted as truth. It would be naive to give credence to others—those constantly preaching the beauties of democracy and human rights, of freedom and justice.

Essentially, it is about resetting the world (dis)order that emerged after the end of the Cold War which lasted from 1947 to 1991. Its culmination was facilitated by the collapse of the Soviet Union, but—as it turns out—it was also a seed of some later conflicts, of which, so far, the drama unfolding around Ukraine is by far the most serious. So far—and let us hope it stays like that, although it does not have to. The great achievement of the dismantling of the USSR was that it was carried out essentially peacefully, owing to the fact that it was principally accepted at the time that all fifteen new post-Soviet republics were enclosed within the borders of the former socialist Soviet republics. And these borders were drawn in a different reality, in the times of the tsarist empire and the Soviet Union, which, after all, was to last forever…

In the Soviet era, it was rather unimportant to whom Crimea or Karakalpakstan, currently an autonomous republic in Uzbekistan, which theoretically has the right to self-determination, was assigned. Going from Tashkent to Samarkand, a part of the road goes through Kazakhstan, because that was the way it was laid out by the logic of the integrated state, the USSR, and now it can cause problems. There are more of them, as Georgia experienced with regard to Abkhazia and South Ossetia, and even earlier with regard to Transnistria, recently recalled more frequently due to its location at the interface between Moldova and Ukraine.

The same three decades have seen the rise of the power of China, which is reshaping the world order, relatively weakening the large and wealthy countries of the West, including especially the US, which does not want to accept it. Although it has been as long as three decades, the rise of China's power is still a shock from which Americans cannot recover. Along the way, several former Third World countries have emancipated themselves. Many of them do not want to forget the humiliation of the colonial era and now refuse to be subjugated by other countries, above all their former imperial metropolises. In this context, the world was in a far-reaching state of geopolitical imbalance and now the great upheaval caused by the Kremlin's regrettable behavior has provoked various demons to leap out from various nooks and crannies. Just as opportunity makes a thief, a major geopolitical crisis makes a chance to pull ahead. So, some are pulling ahead, saying they are all about peace and tranquility.

There are also controversial views being heard suggesting that the West not only wants to at least slow down, if blocking is already impossible, the rise of superpower China and to marginalize Russia on the global stage but that there is also a game being played within the Western powers to strengthen the influence of ones at the expense of others. In particular, the United

States and the United Kingdom walking alongside them, especially after Brexit and the turning away from the European Union, under the slogans of confronting Russia and countering the alleged threat from China to the stability of international relations, are seeking to reduce the relative economic weight of the European Union, especially its regional powers—Germany and France. According to such views, anti-Russian sanctions—above all cutting off the West's imports of oil and gas from Russia, which comes very easily to the Americans and the British, as they have imported little of these energy carriers from there[1]—are also used by the US to increase Europe's economic dependence on them by structurally tying it to buying these raw materials at exorbitant prices from US suppliers. Such views are hardly convincing, but it would be no less convincing to assume that the US energy lobby and politicians who are servile toward it are not exploiting the situation for vested interests at the expense of worsening the position of their European allies and partners.

Thus, we have the Second Cold War gaining momentum, only with a few spots of hot wars. I have been describing the state of tension in international relations as the Second Cold War for some time. Already in 2014, international relations, especially those on the West–East line, had deteriorated enough to allow the use of such a term: "100 years ago the war was provoked. It lasted almost four and a half years and millions of people were killed. In the beginning, no one knew it would be a world war, but it quickly took such a character. In the 1920s and 1930s, it was called the Great War. Only when 25 years later another war had broken out, the one occurring since 1914 to 1918 became called the First World War. Shortly after the end of the Second World War, that of 1939–1945, the Cold War was started. It was unleashed by the West against the East, which was defeated after a couple of decades. On this occasion, it even happened that "the end of history" was announced after 1989. How early…

It took only one generation of peace time before the initiation of a Second Cold War. Since now the confrontation of the years 1946–1989 will be called by historians the First Cold War. However, this time it won't be won by the party which has started it, that is again by the West. It won't be won by the East either. The winner will be China, that is taking care of her business and consistently reforming and developing the economy, which strengthens the Chinese international position every year. After a dozen more years—when foolish Second Cold War hawks will be tired, both in the US and its allies, and in Russia—China will be even a greater power. Both, absolutely and in comparison with the US, the European Union, Russia… Relatively also much better will be the position of other countries, including the emancipating economies, which are smart enough that do not get involved in the winds of the next cold war."[2] These are phrases written eight years earlier than this text, but I believe they remain their validity. I now believe that it may well be that China will not so much win this Cold War as emerging from it less battered, i.e. in a relatively more favorable shape than other "frontline" countries.

2014 was an important year, perhaps even a watershed year due to Ukraine's anti-Russian turn following the Maidan protests, described by some even as a revolution, and due to Russia's annexation of Crimea. However, the reasons not so much for the outbreak as for the gradual spawning of the new Cold War have their origins a full decade earlier. The American invasion of Iraq—American, albeit with US allies involved—marked the beginning of a breakthrough in Russia–West relations, especially Russia–US relations, because they were still good with Germany, also because they did not join the UN unsanctioned invasion of Iraq. This was when the process of reviewing Russia's position began, leading to a shift away from cooperation with the West to "getting up from its knees," to which Russia was supposedly thrown after the liquidation of the USSR during the years of Boris Yeltsin's presidency. This was fostered by the de facto failure of the US policy in the Middle East. From the Kremlin's perspective, the importance of the White House must have declined in the world, so how could it not take advantage of such a situation? The reasoning of the kind—the weaker the partner or adversary, the stronger I am—made itself known in many aspects of Russian policy. By the way, it is similar to the current anti-Russian and even more so anti-China policy of the US.

In the rich West, especially on both sides of the North Atlantic and on the western shore of the North Pacific, an increasingly powerful, because more economically developed, China is seen as a threat to their interests, although it is said to be a threat to the stable world order. If the answer to such a real or illusory threat is not wasting resources on increased military spending, but on economic programs that compete with Chinese initiatives, then fine. According to rough calculations, during the ten years of the BRI—from its initiation in 2013 until 2022—China committed more than USD 900 billion to the project. And it is only after these ten years that the rich and large countries grouped in the G7 pledged at their summit at the end of June 2022 to mobilize over the next five years USD 600 billion, 200 of which from the US, from private and public sources for investment in underdeveloped countries. This idea, called Partnership for Global Infrastructure and Investment, PGII, according to statements by G7 officials, is not meant to be a rival to the BRI, but in a way complement it by directing money both to hard infrastructure such as roads and bridges, ports and airports, as in the Chinese

14 The Second Cold War is a World War

initiative, and to climate projects as well as energy security, digital connectivity, health and women's equality. In some of these domains, the Chinese have already been active in many countries for several years, so it remains to be seen how competitive the PGII will be in relation to the BRI, and how much both initiatives will unanimously support the economic development of the lagging countries.

In poor countries, China is looked upon with the hope of helping them develop, but there is also plenty of concern that cooperation with such a large and powerful partner cannot be balanced and based on partnership. So while some put high hopes on China—with its hybrid political–economic system, which I call Chinism,[3] and which consists of skillfully combining the power of the invisible hand of the market with the visible hand of the state and the rule of meritocracy—others fear and warn against it. Such Sino-skepticism is bad for globalization because it depresses an already insufficiently mature political globalization. While the West's more than restrained attitude toward China during Maoism could be understood, it is difficult to applaud it in the times of Chinism.

During the First Cold War "Maoism exercised a particular attraction for underdeveloped, colonized or recently decolonized states as Tanzania, Nepal, India, Cambodia and Indonesia, which at least superficially seemed to resemble pre-1949 China. It exercised this appeal often without much material aid from the PRC, certainly in comparison with the budget dispensed by the Soviet-sponsored Comintern through the 1920s and '30s. In true guerilla style, Mao's ideas and saying have captivated the developed world too, percolating through the best French arrondissements and elite US campuses—«Dig deep tunnels, store grain everywhere», declaimed radical Harvard students in the 1970s. Maoism has also taken root in parts of the developing world that bear no solid resemblance to pre-revolutionary China—such as Peru. Without a proper understanding of Maoism's global appeal and travels, it is hard to make sense of events as geographically and chronologically disparate as the Malayan Emergency, the 1965 massacres in Indonesia, the cultural revolutions of Western Europe and the US of 1968, the Vietnam War and the Khmer Rouge genocide, the end of white rule in Southern Rhodesia and the rise of Robert Mugabe's ZANU, Shining Path's insurgency in Peru, the civil war in Nepal that ended centuries of monarchy, and contemporary insurrection in India's jungles. Conflicts and crises influenced by Mao are not only major historical events; several are still with us, in India, Peru, Nepal and Zimbabwe."[4] Yet, Chinism has nothing in common with Maoism apart from the territory in which it was born. One of the salient features of Maoism was its "exports", but is this the case with Chinism? Mao Zedong's slogans were popular in the West, but the Xi Jinping's slogans are at best repeated only in China, to create a cult of a leader, but without such emotional involvement as over a third of a century earlier in the case of his paramount predecessor.

Chinism is not the same as the past export of the revolution. Unless one considers as a symptom of such a similarity the possibility of spreading of Chinism in certain regions of the world due to its economic attractiveness and in view of the disillusionment experienced by the people of many poor countries in the face of the economic flaws of democracy, as recently felt in countries as diverse as Bangladesh and Chile, Sri Lanka and Tunisia, South Africa and Haiti. Maoism had practically nothing of creative value to offer, whereas Chinism may be associated with capital accumulation, technology transfer or human capital training. If anarchization continues in the wake of various economic and political crises, if new nationalism develops, if resentment for a strong-arm rule grows, could there be a spillover of Chinism similar to the spread of Maoism half a century earlier? This is something that some in the West may fear and are therefore inclined to confront the Chinese power in advance. This dissonance is yet another factor contributing to the current Cold War.

Now it extends even to the ends of the world, especially to the Arctic. The climate's warming is causing the melting of the ice cap, making more areas of the Far North available for exploration of valuable resources, and more waters for year-round navigation. So not only all the countries bordering the Arctic—Russia, the USA, Canada, Denmark, to which Greenland belongs, Iceland, Norway, Sweden and Finland, but also China, which establishes scientific and research stations and bases there, are becoming active, counting also on a more intensive use of the northern shipping lanes leading from Asia to Europe. In this context, it is not surprising that under the Cold War atmosphere, Russia and the US are aiming at further militarization of the Arctic regions close to them, but the activation of NATO may be surprising. The pact has not yet changed its name to the North Atlantic and Arctic Treaty Organization, NAATO, but this North Atlantic is stretching further, beyond the limits of the North Atlantic proper.

If China and Russia are indeed a threat to the West, then there is a need to react, as NATO Secretary General Jens Stoltenberg stated at the end of August 2022, during his visit paid together with Canadian Prime Minister Justin Trudeau to Cambridge Bay in the Canadian Nunavut province: "Beijing and Moscow have also pledged to intensify practical operation in the Arctic. This forms part of the deepening strategic partnership that challenges our values and our interests."[5] And as we know, challenges need to be answered by action—especially those related to interests, because those related to values are mostly talked about—so China and Russia, in turn, surely will respond to this next American and NATO challenge. Thus, the Cold War is fought in all climatic zones—from the tropics to the Arctic.

The Second Cold War is a world war because, although only a few dozen countries are actively involved, it passively affects everyone, not only due to the rising prices of food and raw materials, especially energy, but also because, in the existing global (dis)order, everyone has to take a position regarding the war in Ukraine. It is impossible not to have an opinion on this matter. It is significant that the issue of Ukraine being militarily attacked by Russia—a permanent member of the Security Council—quickly got into the forum of the UN General Assembly. What also matters is the outcome of the vote on the resolution condemning Russia's wicked act. In the West, it was rightly exposed that as many as 141 countries have condemned Russia. The fact that as many as 52 countries did not support the resolution was highlighted by Russia itself—and in a few other specific places around the world.[6] Only five opposed it, the others abstained from taking a position—notably China proclaiming neutrality, but still showing at least slight pro-Russian inclinations, and India, also taking a basically neutral position, but this time with slight Russoskeptic inclinations.

Israel, Saudi Arabia and Turkey voted in favor of the resolution but did not join the sanctions. Iran abstained, but not only did it not support them, but is even supplying Russia with its *EagleEye* drones, which can be tested in confrontation with the drones sent to Ukraine by Turkey. These Iranian ones were already being used by Yemen's Houthi rebels to attack targets in Saudi Arabia, which President Biden visited in mid-July, stopping there for talks in Israel and the West Bank territory, where he spoke of the Palestinians' right to their own sovereign state.[7] A few days later, President Putin visited Iran, where, in Tehran, he met not only with the hosts, Iranian Supreme Leader Ayatollah Ali Khamenei and President Ebrahim Raisi, who are repaying Russia for arms exports to their country with drone deliveries, but also with Recep Erdogan, President of Turkey, a NATO member that is rearming Ukraine. Of course, everyone was talking about peace and, more specifically, about armaments and energy supplies that are supposed to ensure it…

We should have no illusions that both at the UN forum and on other occasions while taking an official position, in addition to important ideas, about which there is a great deal of noise, there are even more important interests about which the noise is quieter. In seeking an answer to the big question: what is it all about? one must not lose sight of either of the two "i's" —ideas and interests—for the contradictions between one and the other are at stake here.

If politics is a game—or, as others want to call it, the art of seizing opportunities—then surely developing countries will want to use the occasion of the current major conflict, the Second Cold War, to their advantage. They did not cause it, but since it is there, it is important to adapt to it in the best possible way. By developing countries, I mean countries that are not considered the rich West (including Japan, South Korea and Singapore, as well as the antipodes, Australia and New Zealand), which are home to a total of seven of the globe's eight billion people. Leaving aside China and India, which play their own global game, and Russia, they produce about 30% of global production. The World Bank ranks economies into four income groups based on the yearly value of gross national income, GNI, per capita calculated in current dollars. These groups are low-income, medium–low, medium–high and high-income economies. The criteria are updated annually on 1 July. Thus, as of the summer of 2022, low-income countries cover countries with extreme poverty with no more than USD 1,085 *per capita*, medium–low is the range of 1,086–4,255, medium–high 4,256–13,205 and high over USD 13,205.[8]

For the rich West, not only all economies with incomes below the "high" thus defined, but also some with "high" incomes are so-called "emerging" markets. According to the nomenclature used by the IMF, not only Indonesia and Mexico or Brazil and Pakistan are emerging, but also Poland and Chile or Hungary and Turkey. I find this term—emerging economies—to be instrumental, if not downright nonchalant, as such a view treats states with their societies and economies not as a subject of development, but as an object on which the mighty of this world can make money. Well, because opportunities to invest and profit—often from financial speculation in now accessible markets—are "emerging", whereas previously such opportunities were either non-existent or severely limited for political and institutional reasons. This is why, for several years now, I have been talking about emancipating economies and societies. For this is what it is all about—to emancipate ourselves culturally, politically and especially economically, in the midst of imperfect but irreversible globalization. People in still developing countries not only want to be freed from poverty, sometimes absolute, another time only relative, but also to enjoy the benefits of socio-economic development, which narrows the gap between them and those living in wealthy countries. It is natural, after all.

The Second Cold War, escalating in the wake of the war in Ukraine, puts emancipating economies in different circumstances than before. In particular, they are embroiled in a clash between the West and the US and China, and now they want to lose as little as possible from this and, when possible, gain as much as possible. The emancipating economies are by no means interested in the security-threatening increasing international tensions, while for their political and business leaders, new challenges and therefore both threats and opportunities are emerging. Taking advantage of these disparate opportunities for their march forward, they are playing out the penetration into their affairs of world powers, especially the conflicted US and China, but also Russia, and courting them. The emancipating economies and societies are therefore concerned with something quite different from the Western powers and states unequivocally taking the anti-Russian side. The war in eastern Ukraine is very far away for them, while their own problems are very close. It is worth bearing this in mind and not being fooled by an exclusively Euro-American point of view.

President Putin is also irreparably damaging his country and its people with his fateful decision to invade Ukraine. Not for a year or two, not for a decade or two, but for much longer they will suffer the consequences of his ill-advised action. There was no cheap blitzkrieg, there is an expensive nightmare that costs more and more. There will not be enough money in the diminishing state coffer to cover the expenses arising from the aggression and its aftermath. And it is impossible to increase revenues by levying taxes on stupidity and credulity, as the Indian philosopher and leader Kautiyla did in antiquity, in the fourth century BC. Such a mechanism may have worked when the wise man ruled over the unwise, but not when the opposite happens. It is the Russian rulers and those who naively trust them, supporting the "special military operation" who should pay the most for the Kremlin's misdeeds, but the whole of Russian society will pay—as it is actually already paying.

President Putin's aim was to strengthen Russia's status in the world and, above all, his position in his own country. As for the former, he miscalculated at the very beginning, already at zero hour. As for the latter, time will tell how hugely mistaken he was. Yet, much is lost—and will be lost even more—by the Russians who are in most cases innocent of the whole row. They lose economically and politically, socially and morally. Today, they can no longer be proud of their country, and they will have to wait a long time—and the lives of many will not be long enough—to have the reason to be proud again. They owe this to their "sage man" from the Kremlin and it will remain a stigma for years to come, even after they forget there was a shortage of fries in the restaurants taken over from McDonald's.

President Putin has surprisingly done a great service to Moscow's enemies—both those with their motives and those tainted by Russophobia. Now both have hard anti-Russian arguments. Such opportunities are not wasted; they will be exploited mercilessly and for a long time. In particular, even better times came for those for whom a limited armed conflict far from their borders is profitable, as it further fuels the already escalating arms spiral. The military–industrial complex and its supporters in politics and the media are having an exceptionally good time; it has not been this good for decades.

Notes

1. Natural gas imported from Russia in 2021 was less than 5% of the British imports of this fuel, and crude oil and its products imported from Russia accounted for less than 8% of American imports. In the case of Germany, gas imports from Russia amounted to as much as 55, and from France to 17%.
2. Grzegorz W. Kolodko, "Blog. Truth, Errors, and Lies: Politics and Economics in a Volatile World, post 2506, November 10, 2014 (https://www.wedrujacyswiat.pl/blog/kolodko/; access 15.07.2022).
3. Grzegorz W. Kolodko, "Socialism, Capitalism, or Chinism?", "Communist and Post-Communist Studies", 2018, Vol. 51, No. 4, p. 285–298.
4. Julia Lovell, "Maoism: A Global History", Vintage Books, New York, 2020, p. 16.
5. Marita Moloney, "United States to appoint first Arctic Ambassador", "BBC News", August 27, 2022 (https://www.bbc.com/news/world-us-canada-62699129; access 27.08.2022).
6. 12 countries did not take part in the vote, 5 were against (apart from Russia, these were Belarus, Eritrea, North Korea and Syria), and 35 abstained.
7. Just three weeks later, there was another wave of escalation in the Israeli-Palestinian conflict. After a number of Palestinian rockets and mortars had been fired at Israel from the Gaza territory ruled by Hamas, Israeli Prime Minister Yair Lapid said that in response "a precise counter-terror operation against an immediate threat" was carried out. At least 44 Palestinians were killed. In turn, the Secretary General of the Palestinian Islamic Jihad, PIJ, Ziyad al-Nakhala said: "We will respond forcefully to this aggression, and there will be a fight in which our people will win. There are no red lines for this battle and Tel Aviv will be under the rockets of the resistance." See: Yolande Knell, Elsa Maishman, "Israel-Gaza: Death toll rises as Israel targets militants", "BBC News", August 6, 2022 (https://www.bbc.com/news/world-middle-east-62445951; access 6.08.2022).

8. Nada Hamadeh, Catherine Van Rompey, Eric Metreau, Shwetha Grace Eapen, "New World Bank country classifications by income level: 2022-2023", The World Bank, Washington, DC (https://blogs.worldbank.org/opendata/new-world-bank-country-classifications-income-level-2022-2023; access 26.08.2022).

15

The More NATO Grows, the Less Secure Europe Is?

Neither Russia nor NATO—nor almost anyone else with common sense and a feeling of responsibility—wants open armed conflicts; not even those far from their backyards. China and other arming states do not want them either. A cold war is enough, a hot one is unnecessary. What is tragic for some, as people die in wars, is also useful because for others, those who provide the tools for the killing parties, it is a unique opportunity to try more and more new weapons. This is also the case this time in Ukraine. Different types of lethal products are being tested: from small ones, such as the Javelins cumulative charge anti-tank armament supplied by the US, the Next Generation Light Anti-tank Weapon, NLAW, from the UK, the Polish portable anti-aircraft missile set Piorun, PPZR, or the drone-carried MAM-L missiles supplied by Turkey, to larger combat equipment such as the British AS-90 howitzers, commonly known as Braveheart, the American M777 or the German PzH 2000. Not everything can be tested in Yemen, where the sides supported by Saudi Arabia and Iran clash in the civil war, with weapons coming mainly in the former country from Western powers and in the latter from Russia and China. It would still be useful to have an armed conflict around Taiwan, because then the indispensable aircraft and warships used in it, which are not being tested in Ukraine, could be tested there. And all of these are easier to be produced at taxpayers' expense and then sold at a considerable profit. That is why these conflicts are needed, that is why it is necessary to create an atmosphere of a cold war amok or even (pre-)war psychosis.

This is particularly beneficial for arms exporters, of which the US is the absolute global leader, but other leading Western countries—in a sequence: France, Germany, the UK and Spain—are also doing lucrative businesses. In this infamous ranking, Russia is second in the world and China fifth. It is worth knowing, however, that while US arms exports increased by 15% in the five years between 2016 and 2020 compared to the period between 2011 and 2015 and their share of global exports reached 37%, Russia's exports fell—yes, fell, not increased—by 22% and its share fell to 20%. While the value of France's military equipment exports increased by as much as 44% during this period, to a level equal to 8.2% of global exports, China's foreign sales fell by 7.8% and its share was only 5.2% from 2016 to 2020, even less than Germany's exports, which accounted for 5.5% of global arms exports. Let us add that the US' main customers are, in a sequence, Saudi Arabia, Australia and South Korea; Russia's are China, India and Algeria; France's are India, Egypt and Qatar; Germany's are South Korea, Algeria and Egypt; and China's are Pakistan, Bangladesh and Algeria.[1]

It would be difficult in democratic states to push through military spending—especially given the paucity of public funding for the social policy—if a great majority of the population, including in particular those occasionally voting in elections, were against it. People are supposed to support such a course of politics, but for this to be possible, they have to be convinced that it is necessary because the enemy is lurking. And it becomes possible with a variety of social engineering techniques to intimidate people and skillful manipulation of public opinion, which politicians and lobbyists find quite easy with the help of the zealous media that willingly foster this for ideological or vested motivations.

We are all persuaded by ideological centers, political lobbies and special interest groups. Today, the most effective, even total instrument of this persuasion are the media—the press, radio and television, and since recently the Internet and various social media. Sometimes all these types of communication are intertwined in the implementation of their educational—or, if you prefer, manipulating human knowledge and awareness—missions. We are all brainwashed, only we wash it in different laundries. I use "BBC World News" and "The Economist", but at least I know what detergents they use. So, it would be good for everyone to become aware of what kind of laundry they use and what means they use to convince us to their own—to their own, not always objective, although it happens as well—reasons. While having numerous disputes and discussions, we can easily sense the programs of which TV station our interlocutor is watching, which radio he is listening to, which newspaper or weekly he is reading, or which internet portals he is surfing.

15 The More NATO Grows, the Less Secure Europe Is?

Sometimes, after just a few sentences, we can see that our American interlocutor is a Fox News viewer, not CNN (or vice versa), that he is a reader of "The New York Post?" and not the "New York Times". Or in Poland, that it is a TV viewer who watches TVP "News", and not TVN "Facts" (or vice versa), or a reader of a daily "Gazeta Polska Codziennie" and not "Gazeta Wyborcza", or a weekly "Sieci" and not "Polityka". Even in Russia, apart from central laundries such as the pro-Kremlin propaganda tubes "TASS" or "RIA Novosti", there are media critical of the Kremlin, such as "Rosbalt.ru" (referred to by the regime as a foreign agent) or "Kommersant" (if someone can read between the lines, and many Russians, especially those experienced during Soviet times, deal with it very well), which have an influence, unfortunately only moderate, on the formation of public opinion.

It happens, unfortunately, that even during academic disputes, even professors do not shine with a profound knowledge of verified facts and their originally thought-out interpretations, but just speak the language of this or that newspaper or television. Listening to someone else's opinion on topics as diverse as the war in Ukraine or inflation, population migrations or global warming, it is not difficult to guess what this person is reading and watching. Unable to avoid using these indoctrination centers—these peculiar brain laundries—it is really worth considering what are the ideas and interests behind the content conveyed to us. Of course, besides a sincere desire to provide us with the truth and nothing but the truth…

It is astonishing how smoothly aggressive propaganda is shaping public sentiments and political opinions. Even in a country with such a peaceful culture and balanced society as Finland, it has succeeded in essentially skewing public opinion in favor of joining NATO, the membership in which does not increase the country's security, as no enemy threatens it, but will certainly force an increase in military spending, at least to that famous NATO 2% of GDP. While a month before the Russian invasion of Ukraine, only 28% Finns supported the idea of joining NATO, in March it was already 62, and in May 76%.

Finland excellently discounted its neutrality during the First Cold War. This occurred mainly because the country was led by an outstanding statesman, Urho Kekkonen—Prime Minister in 1950–1956 and President in 1956–1982. As a result of his pragmatic strategy and the politics of the so-called Finlandization, this country, still very poor in the late 1940s, experienced significant economic growth. Thanks to cleverly structured relations with both the West and the East, especially the Soviet Union , living standards increased faster there than in the West European countries. While, for example, in Belgium in the years 1950–1982, GDP (in 2017 US dollars) increased by 221%, in Finland, growing on average by 0.8% points faster, by 4.4%, it increased by 314%. This is a big difference for European capitalist economies and a third of a century.

Now it is not only in this northern country that this class of statesmen is absent. Instead, there is Prime Minister Sanna Marin, supporting Finland's accession to NATO, who tries to get rid of the attacks of the political opposition and nosy media caused by some video clip circulated on the web, in which she plays and dances, as she says, as other young people do. The accompanying very solemn public debate prompted her to take a test to prove that she was not under the influence of drugs, which, as she assures, she did not use even when she was a teenager, so not so long ago, since at 36, she is the youngest head of government in Europe. Prime Minister Marin also admitted that the photo, captured inside her mansion and showing topless two well-known influencers, which got viral on the web, is "not appropriate" and apologized for it. Can anyone imagine something similar in Kekkonen's time?!

This is all in the context of Russia invading Ukraine and telling people that if they do not arm themselves, it can invade them too. If this was indeed true, then yes—one should strengthen oneself in military terms to a level that guarantees deterrence of a potential aggressor. But it is more than doubtful that this is true. Isn't it the case, one might ask, that the more NATO grows, the less secure Europe is? Finland's joining NATO means that its troops will be if not a stone's throw, then the boom of a gunshot away from St. Petersburg. If NATO's greatest concern is the presumption that Russia could attack some of its member states, then—sensible analysts and security experts ask—why keep poking Russia with the expansion of the NATO territory to Russian borders?[2] European security can only be guaranteed in cooperation with Russia and not by fueling a mutual arms race.

Various assumptions can be made about the political-military intentions of significant states or their associations, but sometimes what is more important is not what they actually are, but what people subjectively think about them and how public opinion is formed against this background, which for its observers and politicians is an objective fact. China is certainly not planning to invade Japan, but some Japanese may have a different opinion on the matter. The US probably has no desire to invade Venezuela, but some of its residents listening to the rhetoric of their President Nicolás Maduro may think otherwise. Russia is not planning an attack on any European Union country, but an astonishing number of citizens in its member states believe the opposite. This is clearly shown by representative surveys. As many as 84%

15 The More NATO Grows, the Less Secure Europe Is? 117

agree with the statement that "The invasion in Ukraine is a threat to the security of the EU", and only 12% of respondents disagree. In turn, 77% believe that "The invasion in Ukraine is a threat to the security of our country", while the opposite is believed by 20%. With such assessments, 73% agree and 20 disagree that "More money should be spent on defense in the EU".[3] If almost three-quarters of those questioned agree to an increase in defense spending, it will be difficult to oppose it. We should have no doubt that the applause would be somewhat more modest if, instead of "defense", the terms "military" or "armaments" spending were used, and much less if the question were to add: "knowing that you will have to pay for it out of increased taxation on your income", but there is a reason not to emphasize that.

However, it is not in the interest of the questioned how not to be afraid and not to agree with the expansion of state military spending when at a local political rally the leader of the ruling party says, and the media are eager to publicize it, that "it is better to spend money and not be occupied than not to spend and then be occupied, destroyed, humiliated, murdered, raped. This is what we have in Ukraine. If we want to avoid that, we cannot pinch pennies."[4] So, we do not. And not only for the military but also (let us hope) for healthcare, where spending is expected to increase to 7% of GDP over the next few years, as assured by the political leader in the same speech. Here by two percentage points of GDP compared with previous years, there by one point, so where—in which sectors of public services, in education or science, in culture or sports, in administration or diplomacy—should they decrease by as much as three percentage points? This is something that politicians are silent about, either because they are afraid to tell people the bitter truth or because they themselves do not understand that they are preaching mutually contradictory promises. Such is the logic (?) of politics, such is the negation of the logic of arithmetic, according to which the sum of all shares in a given whole equals that whole, for some shares cannot grow without a corresponding decrease in others.

Both chambers of the Polish Parliament, the Sejm and the Senate, passed "The Law on Defense of the Fatherland" increasing the share of military expenditure in GDP to 3% from 2023 onwards without a single dissenting vote. It is difficult to believe that such unanimity is genuine, and credence must probably be given to those who say that those with different opinions did not have the courage to demonstrate their objection by voting in the face of the strong pressure exerted on them. Instead of shouting loudly about it, they are whispering quietly.

This one percentage point more than the NATO recommendation to spend 2% GDP on defense—a recommendation, not a formal obligation—in the realities of 2023 is equal to around 33 billion zlotys. According to the government's draft budget, in 2023, GDP is to increase in real terms by only 1.7%. Due to the expected increase in prices by 8.1%, it gives a nominal GDP of 3.32 trillion zlotys.[5] Military spending, which automatically grows to at least 3.0% of GDP under "The Law on Defense of the Fatherland" adopted five months earlier, increases by 0.8% points of GDP, while health care expenditure only by 0.25% points. In order to have as much as 100 billion zlotys in the budget for military expenses, other expenses must be limited or even cut in real terms, which can be very difficult, and with regard to public services sometimes quite impossible in democratic conditions. It is possible to increase taxation on households and entrepreneurs, but then it is difficult to win elections, and furthermore, fiscalism is already large enough and its further expansion could turn against economic development. So, the easiest way—and this is what the authorities of many countries following a similar path will resort to—is to increase the budget deficit and public debt with all its consequences, which will become increasingly onerous with rising interest rates.

Anglo-American military hawks, speaking through the media, which they unquestionably influence, are encouraging in various ways to increase military spending. As is well known—someone's expenditure is someone else's income. And so, with increasing frequency, the public narrative concerned about "security" includes anti-Beijing themes dedicated to Taiwan that "should continue to provide military training to all men (and why not women, too?) and create a territorial defense force. It should also increase its military budget, which stands at about 2% of GDP—low for a country in such danger (Israel spends 5.6%)."[6] Sure, ideally everyone should spend so much. Not some 2–3%, as in some, leading in terms of armaments, countries of NATO, whose Secretary General, at the "historic" and "landmark" Madrid summit at the end of June 2022, declared that 2% of GDP was only the lower limit of desirable defense spending, but perhaps 3–4 or even more would be better? The more, the better; only then it will be safe…

Well, no. There may indeed be exceptional cases where it will be safer somewhere, but in the vast majority of cases it will be just as safe as before, only for a lot more public money, or it will even be less safe because of the increase in international tensions caused by the ratcheting up of the arms race. After all, if NATO countries arm themselves even more than before, Russia will do the same. As well as China, of which confrontational Jens Stoltenberg spoke at the Madrid NATO summit that during the meetings "the challenges

Beijing poses to our security, interests and values"[7] were discussed. And he says so when, over the past few years, the already roughly threefold higher US military spending has grown faster than China's.

The trick is to balance military—or, if someone prefers, defensive—forces with as low an input level as possible, rather than increasingly higher. One should not be a naïve pacifist, but neither should one be an unwise militarist. The distance between pacifism and militarism can sometimes be much greater than between 1 and 2% of defense/war expenditure, but surely the lower the cost level at which relative balance is achieved, the better. Despite greater production and with almost twice the population, total military spending by 2022 in 32 European countries, 28 of which are NATO members and four EU members outside NATO, was half that of the US. The Europeans in NATO spent only 1.7% of GDP on their armed forces, relatively less than half than the Americans. And they were doing the right thing, especially Germany spending 1.5, Italy 1.4 and Spain just 1%. Now, even Germany is planning to raise its military budget to 2% of GDP. It is astonishing, and some time ago it was completely unimaginable, that joy could prevail in Poland over the fact that Germany is arming itself…

In the atmosphere of the arms race between the Western and Eastern powers, many other countries will increase their armaments, including developing poor countries, to which the most powerful are eager to supply new (but often not the latest) weapons, often on credit, increasing their debts. In all countries, this absorbs additional resources, diverting them from other legitimate objectives. In extreme cases, over-armament can be accompanied by poverty and hunger, as in pathological North Korea and some African countries; in countries at twice the world average level of development, such as Poland, the lack of resources to improve the material conditions of teachers; in economies at the highest level of development, such as the United States, weak support with public pennies for health care for millions of uninsured citizens.

This makes Pope Francis all the more right when, in a situation where the provision of elementary needs is seriously underfunded, he calls the raising of arms expenditure madness: "I was ashamed to read that a group of countries agreed to raise arms spending to 2% of GDP in response to what was happening. Madness (…) the real answer is not more weapons, more sanctions and political-military alliances, but a different way of managing the world; not by showing teeth."[8] He was met with a sharp retort for this and we immediately learned that Francis was behaving "like leftists once sponsored by the USSR."[9]

Thus, contrary to common sense, but in keeping with the stupidity of some and the thriving interests of others, the world is spending more and more on armaments—already topping USD 2 trillion by a rapidly growing margin—although it should be spending less and less. Even though the overwhelming majority of weapons will never be used in any military clashes, the burgeoning arms race will contribute to the deaths of millions of people. This will happen because of climate change, because that is how the coupling between the economy, politics and the environment works.

Notes

1. "SIPRI Arms Transfers Database", Stockholm International Peace Research Institute (https://armstrade.sipri.org/armstrade/page/toplist.php; access 5.07.2022).
2. Zhou Bo, "The war in Ukraine will accelerate the geopolitical shift from West to East", "The Economist", May 14, 2022 (https://www.economist.com/by-invitation/2022/05/14/senior-colonel-zhou-bo-says-the-war-in-ukraine-will-accelerate-the-geopolitical-shift-from-west-to-east; access 13.05.2022).
3. "Key Challenges…", op. cit.
4. "Jarosław Kaczyński…", op. cit.
5. The 8.1% index is for the GDP deflator. The consumer price index, CPI, is expected to be 9.8, and the producer price index, PPI, as much as 13.2%. In 2023, according to the government's forecasts and plans, all three indicators are expected to remain at a similar level and amount to 4.6, 4.8 and 4.0%, respectively. "Budget Act for 2023. Justification", Council of Ministers, Warszawa, August 30, 2022 (https://www.gov.pl/web/finanse/projekt-przekazany-do-rds4; access 31.08.2022).
6. "How to deter China from attacking Taiwan", "The Economist", April 23, 2022 (https://www.economist.com/leaders/2022/04/23/how-to-deter-china-from-attacking-taiwan; access 14.09.2022).
7. Frank Gardner, "NATO summit: Five challenges for the military alliance", "BBC News", June 28, 2022 (https://www.bbc.com/news/world-61924778); access 28.06.2022).
8. "Papież: podniesienie wydatków na zbrojenia do 2 proc. PKB «szaleństwem»" ("Pope: raising spending on armaments to 2 percent. GDP is «madness»"), "PCh24.pl", March 24, (https://pch24.pl/papiez-podniesienie-wydatkow-na-zbrojenia-do-2-proc-pkb-to-szalenstwo/?utm_source=rss&utm_medium=rss&utm_campaign=papiez-podniesienie-wydatkow-na-zbrojenia-do-2-proc-pkb-to-szalenstwo); access 31.03.2022).
9. "Papież Franciszek niczym lewacy sponsorowani kiedyś przez ZSRR. Wojna w Europie, a on krytykuje wydatki na zbrojenia" ("Pope Francis like leftists once sponsored by the USSR. War in Europe, and he criticizes military spending"),

"Najwyższy czas!", March 24, 2022 (https://nczas.com/2022/03/24/papiez-franciszek-niczym-lewacy-sponsorowani-kiedys-przez-zsrr-wojna-w-europie-a-on-krytykuje-wydatki-na-zbrojenia/; access 31.03.2022).

16

Nostalgia for Authoritarian Regimes Sets In

Since 1980, the frequency of heat waves, which the World Meteorological Association, WMA, defines as at least three consecutive days with temperatures clearly above the long-term average, has increased 50-fold. In this respect, the situation is different in different parts of the world. The WMA experts estimate that in a particular region of India, where 400 million people live, heat waves will last longer and will happen 32 times more often than they occurred at the end of the twentieth century. Almost half of the population engaged in some kind of occupation in agriculture, crafts, trade and services, works in the "fresh" air. But when the heat exceeds 40 °C, one can't work normally. In Europe, even in the Mediterranean countries, it is not that bad, although there also happen temperatures above 40 °C there. So far, for example, in Spain, air conditioning standards for public and commercial buildings have been set at a minimum of 27 °C.

Two-thirds of Europe is affected by severe drought, which is perhaps the worst such event in 500 years. A report by the Global Drought Observatory, GDO, published in the middle of the 2022 summer, has warned that it affects yields and triggers fires. Severe droughts are lasting several months longer in some southern European regions than elsewhere in the continent. There will be no hunger, but the prices of some crops are likely to be higher, as the European Union forecast a decline in maize yields by 16, soybeans by 15 and sunflower by 12% compared to the average of the previous five years. "The latest update of the Combined Drought Indicator, CDI, including the first ten days of August 2022, points to 47% of Europe being in warning conditions and 17% in alert conditions. Soil moisture and vegetation stress are both severely affected. Drought hazard has been increasing, especially in: Italy, Spain, Portugal, France, Germany, the Netherlands, Belgium, Luxembourg, Romania, Hungary, northern Serbia, Ukraine, Moldova, Ireland and United Kingdom. The rest of Europe, already affected by drought, maintains stable severely dry conditions. Local recovery is observed in southern Czech Republic, northern Austria, and limited areas of central France. Regions already affected by drought in spring 2022 (e.g., northern Italy, south-eastern France, some areas in Hungary and Romania), are the ones with the most worsening conditions."[1]

We continue to burn—we, the mankind—in our global furnace, emitting a mass of greenhouse gases that contribute to life-threatening global warming. Like a man, who despite warnings that this habit puts him at risk of deadly cancer, continues to smoke cigarettes. Preventing the catastrophe of climate overheating—an existential threat to humanity—requires a 43% reduction of carbon dioxide, CO_2, emissions in the 2020s decade. This is what the experts of the UN research body, International Panel on Climate Change, IPCC, estimate.[2] This was also the goal set at the global Climate Change Conference, COP26, in Glasgow in November 2021. Just six months later, the same IPCC was already sounding the alarm that the path we were on was leading not to a decrease in emissions but to an increase of 14% by 2030. This is a recipe for civilizational suicide (homicide?) in a more distant time horizon, a few generations from now, but it could happen so, because already the temperature of the Earth, as measured by the IPCC, is 1.3 °C higher than it was two hundred years ago when the first Industrial Revolution sparked. Keeping the global temperature rise below 1.5 °C requires reaching a peak in CO_2 emissions by 2025, according to climate scientists and environmentalists. After that, it should absolutely decrease. There is no way it can happen; we have missed the opportunity in the pursuit of income growth, but perhaps we can achieve this desired breakthrough a few years later?

Unfortunately, the opportunity that emerged after the COP26 is now rapidly being thwarted by the new arms race. The COP27 taking place in autumn 2022 in Sharm el-Sheikh has been yet another convention of anxious climate politicians and environmentalists, yet another cry for restraint, but will the legitimate concerns continue to be pushed into the shadows by the powerful influence of militarists? Unfortunately, this seems so, because despite what is being discussed and suggested not only at successive COPs, it is not investing in environmental protection and climate stabilization that is rapidly increasing but in armaments. The flight of the moth to the flame continues…

The environmental-climate crisis is the biggest problem facing humanity in the twenty-first century, which is still not being solved effectively. It is bad, and the last few quarters have made it even worse. It may turn out that it is impossible to tackle global warming democratically and peacefully without cutting military spending. Meanwhile, the recent period shows that a dramatic mistake is being made, that the irrational policies of institutions as diverse as the Kremlin and the White House are pushing us in the wrong direction. The so-called defense spending is supposed to defend us against enemies—so often illusory, because there are none, so they have to be invented—but in the process, we deprive ourselves of the resources necessary to defend ourselves against the greatest of all real enemies, the climate cataclysm.

In numerous places on the planet, the warming of the climate will deprive many people of the conditions not only for a decent but for any kind of life. Unacceptable inequalities—income, wealth and social inequalities—will worsen. Some people, in order to survive, will flee poor countries and, as a consequence, large migrations to richer countries will increase exponentially, while these richer countries may not be able to cope with the influx of masses of refugees in a civilized manner. Other people will demonstrate in the streets, incite uprisings and revolts, and some in extreme cases will resort to terrorist acts. There will be no time for democracy, there will be pressure for autocracy as a response to anarchization.

For a variety of reasons—one of which, unfortunately, being the shortcomings of democracy, which is deficient not only in institutionally weak states with a lack of mature political culture—nostalgia for authoritarian regimes sets in. Where ineptitude in governance leads to economic, social and political destabilization, the ground for anarchization is laid. In the short term, the response is usually an authoritarian regime, often military, as we see in some countries in Asia and especially Africa, and which, to the surprise of many, may also occur on other continents.

In Chile, it was supposedly a great achievement of democracy that, after mass protests, a large, pluralist commission was set up to draft a new constitution that would guarantee full democracy, unlike the constitution adopted in 1980 under the dictatorship of Augusto Pinochet. In a national referendum on September 5, 2022, this proposal was decisively rejected; as much as 61.9% voted against its adoption and only 38.1 were in favor. Probably the obligation to participate in the vote contributed to the fact that even those who had even slight doubts about the submitted text decided not to accept it, assuming that they would like the new version more. Such can be the consequences of direct democracy. No wonder, because the project consisted of as many as 388 articles containing something nice for everyone, often without sufficient precision of the legal language required of basic law, to the extent that even some genuine supporters of democracy have called for its rejection, because what to do with provisions such as, for example, that the central bank—one of the few institutionally good structures—is to retain its independence, but its powers and responsibilities are to be extended to include "employment protection, care for the environment and the natural heritage".

In contrast, in an institutionally strong democracy, where the principles for balancing conflicting rationales, *checks-and-balance*, seem to work well, in the United States, it is pointed out that Congress, i.e. the people's elected representatives sitting in the Senate and the House of Representatives, do not represent the people's opinion on important issues. This is the case with regard to the law regulating the possibility of aborting pregnancies or the rules governing gun ownership, where the majority of Americans have a different opinion from their representatives. Even staunch supporters of the American democracy notice these serious political dissonances: "If a woman in Texas has an abortion she is breaking the law, even if her pregnancy is the result of a rape. The same woman may, however, buy an AR-15 rifle capable of firing 45 rounds a minute, and she may carry a pistol on her hip when picking her toddler up from pre-school. In these, and in a few other ways, America is an outlier compared with other rich democracies. You might assume that this simply reflects the preferences of voters. You would be wrong: it is the result of a political failure."[3] Exactly right—this is a major systemic failure. There are more of them. Wyoming with slightly over half a million inhabitants has two senators in the Senate, the same number as California with more than 39 million inhabitants. A peculiar institution of American democracy—the 'filibuster', or parliamentary obstruction—is being used to block bills submitted to Congress, and this can be done by 41 senators, representing just 10% of the electorate, out of the entire 100-seat Senate. Formally, this one-tenth can prevent the adoption of a bill that is supported by senators representing 90% of the society. Quite common is gerrymandering, i.e. manipulation of electoral district boundaries by the ruling majority in order to maintain its power despite the lack of majority support. According to the Brennan Center for Justice, in 2021, in 19 states, mostly governed by Republicans, legislatures have enacted 34 pieces of legislation imposing electoral restrictions aimed at reducing the number of citizens participating in elections. In particular, it is about discouraging African–Americans and Latinos, who mostly vote for Democrats. This population likes to vote on Sundays, after church services, so in Georgia, for example, counties have been empowered to exclude voting on Sundays, an option some are eagerly taking advantage of. And where possible, for example in Florida, a ban was introduced on giving water to thirsty people waiting in line at the polls in the heat so that they would not want to suffer on their way from church on election Sunday. Experts on the American political scene have no doubt that the constitutional 'government by the people' principle has always been a fiction, while some even claim that the reality is closer to the principle of 'one dollar, one vote' rather than 'one person, one vote'.

It is true that for every action there is a reaction. If left-wing pragmatism in the form of a social market economy is revitalized in response to disappointing neoliberalism, as some Latin American societies might hope—Chile after the election of President Gabriel Boric, Colombia after the electoral victory of Gustavo Petro, Peru after the election of Pedro Castillo or Brazil after the return to power of Inácio Lula da Silva—that is a good thing. If, on the other hand, populism grows, that is a bad thing. One has to be careful when making judgments and drawing conclusions and be aware that in the heat of ideological and political clashes, any left-wing orientation is often referred to as populism because it has a bad connotation and is even an invective for some.

The enemy of our enemy does not make him our friend. Worse; we now have two enemies: an incompletely eradicated neoliberalism which, through poor regulation of the economy and biased manipulation of the system and fiscal policy, serves to enrich a few elites at the expense of the many masses,[4] and a populism, which promises much more than it can provide, which distributes national income faster than it creates it, and which wins public applause with empty promises. There are more of these enemies because, in response to the failure of liberal democracy to address social and environmental problems, which require strong social cohesion, deep divisions and antagonistic fractures in societies occur.

In more than one case, election results are contested by the defeated candidate and his—or her, as in the case of Peruvian presidential candidate Keiko Fujimori—political supporters. This is what happened in Peru in 2021, where only 21% of the population was satisfied with the democracy, and it was what happened in Kenya a year later when William Ruto won the election with 50.5% of the vote. Two and a half years earlier, in the spring of 2019, it happened there that the elections were annulled and held again, as in Malawi that same year, when the Constitutional Court annulled the elections due to numerous irregularities in their conduct. While the rare act of invalidating a fraudulently conducted election may itself be considered a sign of democracy, the much more frequent manipulation and irregularities in election procedures contradict it. Sometimes with dramatic consequences, as in the case of

Kenya, where after the 2007 elections at least 1,200 people lost their lives in the riots and 600,000 had to abandon their homes and flee. Ruling in Angola since its liberation from Portuguese colonialism in 1975, the left-wing party, the Angolan People's Liberation Movement, MPLA (Port. Movimento Popular de Libertação de Angola) under President João Lourenço, democratically won another five years in power, but with a much more modest majority than before. In the parliamentary elections at the end of August 2022, it won just over half of the votes—51.17%. Of course, the opposition led by the UNITA party questioned this result.

It is becoming quite common to follow the disgraceful example of the loser American president Donald Trump. When in power, he had weakened the functionality of some institutions of a democratic state, and later, still dividing American society into two hostile factions, described his successor as "an enemy of the state". Now Trump doesn't want to "Make America Great Again!" Now he just wants to "Save America!" from the state's domestic enemies…

In countries with weak political institutions, where the law is not necessarily respected, new authoritarianism can be born. I remember how, a quarter of a century ago, in 1997, in the corridors of a seminar held somewhere in the English countryside, Uganda's President Yoveri Museveni, who came to power in a military coup in 1986 and is still in power even now, as I write these words, tried to convince me that in his country, or in other African countries, democracy did not stand much of a chance, because the votes would go along tribal lines rather than according to political agendas. Therefore, strong, centralized governments of those who know what people need and, of course, know how to provide it, are better. It happened that the rule of Museveni, who has consistently been elected President of Uganda in not necessarily democratic elections, often boycotted by the opposition, most recently in 2021, has proved to be one of the most effective on the African continent; it does not matter much that he used to be a general, it helps a little that he is an economist, at least by education. It now turns out that ethnic differences are actually not needed at all for "tribal" clashing in the political struggle. Charismatic leaders who are able to encourage the masses to follow them, dividing the societies internally, but with a desire to rule everyone, are enough. This antagonizing is sometimes an instrument for moving toward new authoritarianism. This can be observed, unfortunately, more and more clearly in many parts of the world, from Brazil and Ecuador through Hungary and Turkey to Bangladesh and Pakistan.

Faced with inefficient decision-making processes resulting in a social mess and economic anomalies, people look to a strong centralized authority.[5] Not in the form of an accountable parliament chosen in fair elections and a technocratic government that respects the law that people understand, but in the form of a strong leader. The growing lack of trust in democracy in more than one country has long-standing causes, but the waves of perturbations triggered by the war in Ukraine spreading around the world may further weaken democracy.

The confusion in socio-economic relations caused by the aftermath of the Russian aggression and anti-Russian restrictions adds fuel to the fire of discontent. Arab countries are a good example of this evil. While a decade ago there were considerable hopes for the progress of democracy emerging from the wave of the so-called Arab Spring, it is now dreamt of by a diminishing proportion of the population there. The events in Tunisia became a symbol of the failure of promoting democracy. It was where the Arab Spring began with the self-immolation of a protester and the wave of protests sparked by this desperate act in 2011, and in July 2022 the Western model of democracy was rejected in a referendum. In place of the constitution adopted in 2014, a new constitution was accepted, under which President Kais Saied, with inclinations toward hardline rule, was given full executive powers, the supreme command of the army and the ability to appoint a government without parliamentary approval. The main opposition parties boycotted the referendum, so it is not surprising that the supporters of a de facto authoritarian regime won, as up to 95% of voters were in favor of the new constitution, albeit with a low turnout of only 31%.

Comparative survey results published in the summer of 2022 show that, for most societies, what is more important than the form of government is its efficiency—it has to be efficient because people are fed up with the mess. Such is the opinion of more than 60% of respondents in Sudan, Morocco and Palestine territories to more than three-quarters in Jordan, Libya, Tunisia and Iraq. Except for Morocco (48%), in all countries surveyed more than half, and in Tunisia, which has enjoyed relative democracy in recent years, as much as 81%, agree that "This country needs a leader who can bend the rules to get things done." In Iraq, on the other hand, where, with the help of some countries, US-British military intervention has been attempting to establish democracy for a dozen years, it is as high as 87%. In all ten countries surveyed between 2019 and 2022, the perception that the economy is weaker under democratic rule has increased markedly—in Jordan by up to two times and in Morocco by as much as three times.[6] This is what happens when there are elements of democracy but not enough meritocracy that co-determines socio-economic development, where power is corrupt and society undisciplined.

Yet, the great illusion is that strong-arm governments can provide it. It does happen, but rarely.

Politics is being brutalized in both democracy and authoritarianism. Both increasingly succumb to irrational emotions in place of pragmatic reason. Such brutalization is more visible in authoritarian regimes, but it is also more common in democracies. Such emotions have a stronger influence on politics in democracies, but they are also not lacking in authoritarian systems. It bodes badly…

In the future, the higher this literal temperature is, also the higher the temperature of social conflicts will be, to the point of a pre-revolutionary boiling, to which the authorities will in many cases respond with force and even more often with restrictions on freedoms and democracy. Moreover, internal conflicts will spill over into international relations, increasing tensions between different countries. There are already more soldiers than border guards on the borders as diverse as the US–Mexico, Venezuela–Colombia, South Africa–Mozambique, Oman-Yemen, Burma–India or Poland–Belarus. Inter-state antagonisms are escalating.

Notes

1. "Drought in Europe. GDO Analytical Report", European Commission, Luxembourg Publication Office of the European Union, August 2022, p. 1.
2. Matt McGrath, "Climate change: Key UN finding widely misinterpreted", "BBC News", April 16, 2022 (https://www.bbc.com/news/science-environment-61110406; access 16.04.2022).
3. "America's new exceptionalism", "The Economist", July 7, 2022 (https://www.economist.com/leaders/2022/07/07/americas-new-exceptionalism; access 12.07.2022).
4. One prominent American economist, criticising neoliberalism from a slightly different angle, also points out that, because of its immanent vices, it must have provoked certain reactions. "It was perhaps inevitable that neoliberalism's excesses—increased inequality, concentration of corporate power, and neglect of threats to the physical and social environment—would trigger a backlash." See Dani Rodrik, "Getting Productivism Right", "Project Syndicate. The World's Opinion Page", August 8, 2022 (https://www.project-syndicate.org/commentary/will-productivism-supersede-neoliberalism-by-dani-rodrik-2022-08?utm_source=twitter&utm_medium=organic-social&utm_campaign=page-posts-aug22&utm_post-type=link&utm_format=16:9&utm_creative=link-image&utm_post-date=2022-08-08; access 10.08.2022).

5. Ben Rhodes, "After the Fall: The Rise of Authoritarianism in the World We've Made", Random House, New York 2022.
6. "Democracy in the Middle East & North Africa", Arab Barometer, July 2022.

17

All Scenarios Are Black, Although the Geography of the Frying Will Vary

There is no point in waiting for years and decades and testing various black scenarios. As far as climate overheating is concerned, all scenarios are black, although the geography of the frying will vary. This must be prevented, and it is still possible to do so. But it is still expensive. So how much is needed in terms of human and material resources? How to finance it? The estimates of the future costs of combating global warming so that the Earth's temperature does not rise by more than the critical 2 °C are highly disjointed depending on who is counting, using which method and for what purpose. To tell the truth, we do not know how much it will cost; we will only find it out in the course of this most difficult human escapade in history.

In the summer of 2022, the US Congress finally passed, and on August 18, President Biden signed the Inflation Reduction Act, IRA. Although this bill deals with an amount five times less than the Democrats originally wanted (President Biden suggested as much as USD 3.5 trillion, and the IRA package is about 740 billion), the American President said it was "one of the most significant laws in our history" and "With this law, the American people won and the special interests lost."[1] The very name of the bill is misleading, and some—especially Republicans—argue that the additional spending triggered by the implementation of the IRA will further fuel inflation. By contrast, the White House maintains that inflation will be lower thanks to lower energy and healthcare costs and a narrowing budget deficit. What is important is that half of the extra public spending in the next ten years, USD 370 billion, will go to the fight against global warming. In particular, the IRA provides tax breaks and funding for renewable energy projects, subsidies for the purchase of electric vehicles and energy-efficient home refurbishments, and offers incentives for companies to invest in technologies that reduce methane emissions. The IRA is to ensure that adequate funds are raised for these glorious purposes—as well as for health insurance subsidies and deficit reduction—from additional taxes, including USD 222 billion in 15% income tax from companies with annual profits of at least USD 1 billion. "The IRA marks a new chapter for America's climate policy. By weaving together a vast array of tax credits, loan guarantees and grants, it will encourage people to make low-carbon purchases, such as of electric cars, and encourage businesses to invest in green technologies. Rhodium Group, a consultancy, predicts it will cut America's net greenhouse-gas emissions by 40% in 2030 from 2005 levels. Without the IRA, the reduction would be 30%. The extra reduction is about two years' worth of British emissions. America will now be working alongside most of the rest of the world in trying to limit global warming—something that would otherwise have been in doubt."[2] Especially this announcement of a willingness to cooperate "with most of the rest of the world" inspires hope. All the more so, one should try not to find China beyond "the rest", especially after China, offended by Nancy Pelosi's visit to Taiwan, rashly suspended cooperation in this matter with the USA. A good opportunity to reactivate the working dialogue on this matter was provided by the COP27 meetings in Egypt and the G-20 summit, a group of 19 large economies and the European Union, held in mid-November 2022 on the island of Bali in Indonesia.

Analytical and research experts from the Swiss Re Institute, a reinsurance company operating around the globe, estimate that if the assumptions made at the Paris UN summit in 2015 about the climate policy leading to the so-called net-zero greenhouse gas emissions in 2050—i.e. a state in which as many gases are absorbed from the atmosphere as are emitted there—were not implemented, the gross world product, GWP (equal to aggregate gross domestic products, GDP) would be 10% smaller in 2050 than it would have been in the absence of climate change. Assuming the current trajectory, proceeding along the path that implies an increase of 2.0–2.6 °C in the Earth's temperature by 2050, GWP could be 11–14% lower by mid-century than in a hypothetical world without climate change. But assuming that decisive actions against climate warming are not undertaken, even worse things could happen than if we follow the current trajectory, and if the temperature rises even further, by 3.2 °C, GWP will be 18% lower than it would be under the stable climate.[3]

Someone may say that these will not be as dramatic losses as they claim. If GWP of just under USD 130 trillion (according to the purchasing power parity, PPP) in 2022 could grow by 2.5% per year on average without climate change, it would double to USD 260 trillion by 2050. Yes, 11–14% less is a huge amount—USD 30–36 trillion—but after all, the value of world production would still be as much as around 75% higher than today. Given the population growth projected for this time from the current level of 8 billion to around 9.7 billion in 2050[4] (over 80 million more people each year), GDP per capita, which is currently at around USD 18,700 according to PPP, as calculated by the World Bank, would reach USD 23,000 instead of USD 26,500. Much worse, but still not yet a disaster.

Well, for some it would be—will be?—a great catastrophe, sometimes even a complete tragedy, because the burdens of these processes will not be spread on the shoulders of people in different parts of the world according to averages. Someone's income may increase by even more than would have happened without the curse of climate change, to somebody else the heated world will collapse on their head. The Swiss Re Institute, using IPCC data and projections, estimates that with an 18% lower GWP in 2050 compared to its hypothetical value in the absence of climate change, it would be about 10% lower on average in developed countries, but as much as half in some economies in Southeast Asia. And yet, behind this already catastrophic average, 50% less than it could be, there are also huge variations—significantly upward, which is something one can live with, sometimes even quite well, and significantly downward, which means that it's time to die.

According to the International Energy Agency, IEA, in order to achieve net zero emissions by 2050, the annual investment in the green energy transition needs to double to five trillion dollars. Where will the 2.5 trillion come from? A considerable proportion of the necessary expenditure will have to be financed from the state coffers, as the private sector will only participate to the extent that it is profitable to it. With various instruments, especially fiscal and pricing instruments, the area of the commercial viability of an unprecedented investment effort has to be expanded and new mechanisms of public–private partnerships and financial assembly involving multiple ownership entities have to be created in this field, but even so, a significant part of the costs will have to be covered using public finances, from budgetary resources. How to find them there if they are to be sucked up by increased arms expenditure?

The market alone will not solve the problem of combating global warming. It must be strongly assisted by the state with its policies and its financial resources. This is extremely complicated and risky both politically and economically. Insurance companies, even the strongest and largest, may not be able to shoulder the burden of insuring against the bankruptcy of companies that cannot comply with the additional financial burden imposed on them by the state due to their use of energy-driven technologies based on the combustion of raw materials that emit greenhouse gases. Already the elimination of coal implies huge costs. "The transition towards a low carbon economy is non-negotiable but has repercussions for asset valuations. It is clear that climate transition risks can have a substantial impact on equity and credit valuations. The sectors most exposed to a global carbon tax include utilities, materials and energy. Introducing a global carbon levy at USD 100 per ton could hit company earnings in those three sectors by 40–80%. Regionally, Asia is again most exposed. The timing and scope of policy decisions will influence the severity of asset value changes."[5] Delaying the decision to introduce a universal CO_2 levy for years does not lead to its avoidance, but postponing the practical application of such an instrument only raises its future costs.

Notes

1. "America's climate-plus spending bill is flawed but essential", "The Economist", (https://www.economist.com/leaders/2022/08/08/americas-climate-plus-spending-bill-is-flawed-but-essential; access 17.08.2022).
2. Ibidem.
3. "The economics of climate change: no action not an option", Swiss Re Institute, Zurich, April 2022.
4. The UN forecast announced on July 11, 2022, on World Population Day, assumes that the global population, which has increased eightfold over the past two hundred years, will rise to 10.9 billion by the end of the twenty-first century. By 2050, the world average life expectancy will increase to 77.2 years. Over the same period, the share of people aged 65 and over in the world's population is projected to increase from the current 10 to 16%. As much as 43% of the growth in the world's population will be born in just five countries: Nigeria, India, Ethiopia, Congo and Pakistan. In 2023, India becomes the most populous country in the world with over 1.4 billion people, ahead of China. See "A world of 8 billion: Towards a resilient future for all – Harnessing opportunities and ensuring rights and choices for all", United Nations, World Population Day, 11 July, 2022 (https://www.un.org/en/observances/world-population-day; access 17.07.2022).
5. "The economics of climate change...", *op. cit.*, p. 26.

18

Where to Get These Billions and Trillions

In the realities of Poland, a poor institutional solution in the form of an Act of Parliament increases the rigid—necessary to be borne by virtue of law—military budget expenditure to 3% of GDP. This is how much, at least, the government must spend each year for as long as the Act is in force, and for other purposes—including environmental protection—it will spend as much as it decides each year. Thus, the level of military spending is set automatically, while other—more important—expenditure is discretionary. In the case of the military, the government cannot say that it does not have the equivalent of 3% of GDP in the budget, whereas with regard to social and anti-global warming objectives, it can say that it does not have as much as is really necessary. This is how social and green transformation spending, while it should be a priority, becomes residual to military spending and other rigid commitments. Moreover, at the beginning of 2023, Polish Prime Minister Mateusz Morawiecki announced an increase in military spending to a record level in NATO, up to 4% of GDP.

By no means a relative amount of public spending on environmental protection, for example in relation to the level of GDP, should be set strictly. Nor for any other purpose, including such important ones as education and health care. The proportions of public finance allocation to alternative objectives should be the result of serious studies as to the importance and urgency of particular social needs and appropriate political compromise on how to resolve inevitable conflicts of group interests in a way that promotes social cohesion and sustainable economic development. Unfortunately, it is the military that is guaranteed a high level of funding in the form of a percentage of national income and it will now be extremely difficult to move away from such a bad solution. This is an example of a policy mistake that is easy to make and extremely difficult to overcome.

In the previous fifty-year period, 1971–2020, the average annual growth rate of gross world product per person was around 1.7%, which means doubling of its level after 40 years. It is likely to be lower in the next fifty years due to, among others, a reduction in the scale of simple reserves, especially the relatively lower transfer of labor forces from agriculture to industry, where labor productivity is higher, and due to weather perturbations. Here, it is important how consumption and investment will interact in the framework of shared national income, while, in the framework of public expenditure, what the relationship between different types of expenditure for competing purposes will be.

If military spending—both current and investment expenditure in this sector in connection with the arms race—is not only to be ever greater in absolute terms but is also to be greater in relative terms, in relation to the financing of social objectives, then the relative consumption level will have to be reduced. Regarding its core part, the one financed by personal income, this will happen by raising taxes, direct and indirect, and by resorting to inflationary taxation, which is, after all, already happening. In relation to publicly funded consumption, this will be done through relatively lower expenditure on social objectives. Since the policy will have to function in such a way that there will nevertheless be no shortage of resources to combat global warming, consumption will have to be moderated even further. Thus, its level will grow slower than the national income in the future. As a result, the standard of living of the population will be at a lower level than it would have been without the unproductive arms race and the enhancement of the military build-up spiral.

If someone says that, after all, the sense of security is also part of the standard of living, an essential one, it is true. The point, however, is—let us reiterate—that such security should be provided in an internationally balanced environment with the lowest possible level of military expenditure. Contrary to the slogans promoted by the military hawks with their political, scientific and media backgrounds, with ever-increasing military expenditure, more and more people are feeling less and less safe.

Where to get these billions and trillions, if objectively other types of public spending will increase at the same time? The nasty COVID-19 pandemic has cut a few quarters off our life expectancy, but the long-term trend toward longer life is sustainable. Although the lifespan will not increase as much as

18 Where to Get These Billions and Trillions

during the past hundred years, more and more of us will approach our own hundred years in the next hundred. This is also very costly. The majority of healthcare expenditure is on the post-working age population, which will be increasing in number and living longer. In many countries, this will put a heavy strain on public spending.

Where to get these billions and trillions when, due to strong inflationary processes, economies have entered a phase of raising interest rates? This will also increase the mandatory liabilities of state budgets, in some countries beyond the limits of their solvency. Even countries as developed and rich as Germany, France, Japan and Italy will feel the additional burden of the inexorably rising costs of servicing public debt. On average, the ratio of public debt to GDP in poor countries is close to 70% and rising. In Latin America, it increased from an average of 58% in 2019, up to 72% in 2021 and continues to increase. Some of them will not be able to handle the rising interest rates. "Among 73 low-income countries eligible for debt relief under a G20 initiative, eight carry public-debt loads which the IMF has deemed to be unsustainable, and another 30 are at high risk of falling into such a situation. Debt problems in these countries pose little threat to the global economy; together, their GDP is roughly equivalent to that of Belgium. Yet they are home to nearly 500 m people, whose fates depend on whether their governments can afford to invest in basic infrastructure and public services. (…) Taken together, then, 53 low- and middle-income countries are already experiencing debt troubles, or are at high risk of doing so. Their economic size is modest—their combined output amounts to 5% of world GDP—but they are home to 1.4bn people, or 18% of the world's population."[1] How can someone fuel the Cold War and encourage poor countries in need to import expensive weapons? Quite a significant part of their current debt came from foreign purchases of mostly unnecessary weapons on credit.

Where to get the resources for education, which is not only a value in itself, but also contributes to socio-economic development through better worker skills and is the most effective way of reducing excessive fertility in poor countries? The less educated girls are, the earlier they become pregnant and the more children they give birth to, whom the family is then unable to support. In rich Norway, where everyone can write and read and education, from primary schools to universities, takes on average as long as 18 years, the first child is born when the mother is 30 years old and there are 183 children for every 100 mothers. In extremely poor Niger, where 65% (among girls 73%) are illiterate, girls become mothers as early as 18 years of age and 100 mothers have as many as 682 children. In Poland, where basically everyone can read and write and education is received for an average of 16 years, the first child is born when the mother is 28 and 100 mothers give birth to 140 children.

Education costs money, but armaments cost too, so there is not enough for schools and learning. The situation is already bad, and it can become even worse. The World Bank estimates that the percentage of 10-year-olds in middle- and low-income countries who cannot read and understand simple stories has increased from 57% in 2019 to around 70 today. Without such elementary skills, it will be difficult for them to find a good job and earn decently.[2] Throughout their hard lives, such a lack of elementary education will deprive them of as much as USD 21 trillion that they could have earned if there were enough resources for a good education now.[3] According to a study by the United Nations International Children's Emergency Fund, UNICEF, a quarter of countries have no plans on how to make up for the learning loss caused by the pandemic.[4] This requires additional funding, but it turns out that there are other more urgent and supposedly more important tasks: armament. This feeds an emigration potential that other, richer countries will then be unable to cope with. In this way, a revolutionary potential is also growing in many parts of the world. This is also how the seeds of local social and political conflicts can sprout, which in many cases later also become intertwined with ethnic and military conflicts.

Although the poorer half of the world's population generates only 10% of greenhouse gas emissions, it is projected that the countries they inhabit will bear as much as 75% of the costs of climate change. This will have wider social implications. The International Organization for Migration, IOM, already warned in a 2014 report that the migrations provoked by these changes could involve up to one billion people by 2050. This is as many people as there were across the globe two hundred years ago. The likelihood of such an incredible exodus now is even greater. For it is not the hawks of NATO, Russia, China and, unfortunately, a number of other rapidly rearming countries who are right, but Inia Seruiratu, Fiji's Defense Minister (note: defense, not environment), speaking at a conference in Singapore on tensions in China–US relations when he said that "Machine guns, fighter jets are not our primary security concern. The single greatest threat to our very existence is climate change."[5] Anyone who has been to Fiji or other South Pacific islands has seen what extra centimeters of sea level mean to the people there. But everyone, especially decision-making politicians who can do something useful about it, must know what the rise in sea level means for billions of people.

China, and especially Russia, will now be even more eagerly than before held responsible for many of our ills, including those completely through no fault of their own, but there is no doubt that Russia's aggression in Ukraine, and more specifically its multifaceted consequences, are introducing many distortions and fractures into the energy transition processes. Certainly, the energy sector in countries exporting energy resources, oil and gas, is doing very well. This war even pays off—both in poor countries such as Angola or Peru and in rich ones such as the Arab Emirates or Norway. In just one quarter, April-June 2022, the Saudi oil giant ARAMCO made record profits of USD 48.4 billion, as much as 90% more than a year earlier. One has to acknowledge that not only OPEC, an organization of 13 oil-exporting countries, but also the so-called OPEC + , where this plus stands for a further 10 formally unaffiliated oil-exporting countries, including—what is important—Russia, is economically interested in the continuation of the conflict in Ukraine because it is financially profitable for it. It is paying off—and paying off greatly—for the United States, which, overtaking Russia, becomes the world's second-largest oil exporter after Saudi Arabia in 2023. In 2021, the US, Russia and Saudi Arabia's shares of total global exports were 8.2, 11 and 15%, respectively. In addition, the US will become the largest exporter of liquefied natural gas, LNG, overtaking Qatar in 2023.

If more expensive energy from the environmentally damaging burning of fossil fuels catalyzes the transition to renewable energy sources, it will once again become clear over time that every cloud has a silver lining. But is this happening? In part, but at the same time, many economies—from Australia to Poland—are keen to turn again to even more harmful coal combustion. Japan does not intend to abandon coal and is developing an expensive technology, the so-called coal gasification, which reduces its CO_2 emissions. In many countries, mainly the richer ones, it is not coal mines that are being commissioned, but investment projects to enable the imports of oil and gas as a substitute for Russian purchases abandoned under sanctions. But to import more gas from, say, Algeria to France, a new pipeline needs to be built quickly under the Mediterranean seabed. At the end of August 2022, investments in gas exploration and export infrastructure were the subject of talks between the French president and an accompanying group of ministers and businessmen in Algiers. Earlier, in May, Italy had signed agreements on the import of gas and electricity from Algeria. In order to quickly import LNG from Angola to Italy, specialized terminals need to be built to allow unloading and a pipeline network to facilitate further distribution of gas. In order not to start transporting gas from Russia to Germany via the barely built Nord Stream 2 offshore pipeline, new fixed or floating transshipment terminals must be built on the German Baltic coast for liquid gas imported from elsewhere. This is all very expensive, and one might be concerned that once the new facilities are up and running, the ambition to switch to renewables will sink a little, because, after all, the expenditure incurred will have to be recouped. And that takes time.

According to Eurostat, in 2020, France imported 7,780 million m^3 of gas from Russia and 3632 million from Algeria, representing 16.8 and 7.8% of its foreign gas purchases, respectively. If the abandoned imports from Russia were to be fully substituted by purchasing gas from Algeria, imports from Algeria would jump by as much as 215%. Is this realistically achievable? Over what period? At the cost of which additional investments in transport infrastructure and logistics? At how much higher prices? And what about other clients also feeding on the illusion that in their case all these questions will be answered satisfactorily? But will there be enough gas in Algeria to meet the radically increased demand? Italy intends to import it from much more distant countries—Angola and the Congo—just in case. Whether such a solution will be cheaper or more expensive remains to be seen, as it is not known how much it will all cost.

Paradoxically, at the same time, a huge wastage is taking place, as Russia has to burn excess gas, which cannot be sold due to sanctions. When the Canadian prime minister and the head of NATO met north of America to discuss the safety and cleanliness of the Arctic, in the north of Russia, close to the border with Finland, large amounts of gas were burned. Analysts from Rystad, the Norwegian energy consulting firm, estimate that more than 4.3 million cubic meters are burned daily there, which is 1.6 billion cubic meters annually, or 0.5% of gas consumption in the EU. This economic waste is accompanied by environmental damage, because combustion emits about 9 thousand tons of carbon dioxide, CO_2, and the soot that is generated may settle on vast areas of the Arctic. It is not as far as it seems from Portovaya, where instead of being compressed and exported via the Nord Stream 1 offshore pipeline to Germany and Western Europe, the gas is unproductively burned, to Cambridge Bay, where Trudeau and Stoltenberg met. When one thinks about the long distances in the North of Eurasia and America and the Arctic, one should have to look at the globe, not at the map.

As a result, instead of accelerating the energy transition beneficial to the fight against global warming, it may slow down. This is one of the likely side-effects of the anti-Russian economic sanctions, which, in general, had to be imposed, but the sense and usefulness of details of some of them are doubtful. This is how the Cold War heats up the Earth's climate. It is therefore not surprising that strong words were used by the UN Secretary-General, António Guterres, when he said in the context of the response to the war in Ukraine that "Investing in new fossil fuels infrastructure is moral and economic madness."⁶ Perhaps the reason to impose a "state of emergency" in Hungary in the summer of 2022 with regard to the regulation of the energy sector was that many Hungarians could consider the decision of Prime Minister Viktor Orban's government to increase coal mining—and in particular to bring into operation the previously closed Matra power plant burning particularly atmospherically damaging lignite—to be such a madness. Thus, in one fell swoop, democratic procedures are being curtailed and measures are being taken that contradict Hungary's international climate commitments. Their case is just a telling example that will, unfortunately, be emulated by other countries, naturally, with all contextual differences.

Someone will say that Hungary is a small country in the middle of Europe. But the United States is a great country somewhat in the middle of the world. President Biden thought about introducing a climate emergency, which would have given him additional power to push through the government's renewable energy implementation program, which he is unable to do because Congress—democratically elected—does not fully support presidential projects.

There will be more and more such and similar cases of democracy being curtailed, circumvented or even violated. The more states spend, i.e. mostly waste, public money on armaments called defense, the less secure there will be and the more the authorities will reach for autocratic methods of governance. For when there are not enough resources, and there will not be, for what is necessary—and the fight for a life-giving climate is and will remain an imperative—politicians will resort to arguments of force in the face of a paucity of the force of arguments. This is a bad omen for democracy, and its increasing dysfunctionality and giving way to autocracy is a bad omen for peace.

It is not the pro-military "peace defenders" who are right, but Secretary Guterres, when he says that precisely "Renewable energy is the guarantor of peace in the twenty-first century."⁷ We only have to be careful to not too easily switch, by manipulating definitions, to the so-called green energy, which is what is happening now since the Parliament of the European Union has decided that not only nuclear energy (rightly so) but also gas counts as a source of green energy. Some would also like to include coal.

If there is no honest public dialogue and no well-programmed educational effort to win majority public support for the increasing use of nuclear energy—and in many countries, a majority of the public is against it because they have come to believe, either by listening to the lobbyists of the traditional energy sectors or under the impulses of accidents that are very rare, that it could be dangerous—then the authorities will resort to forcing it through in an undemocratic way.

Thus, the Second Cold War, stimulating the very costly arms race, seriously reduces the chances of success of the fight against climate warming. It is still possible, guided by wisdom, reason and social sensitivity, to win it peacefully and democratically, but the chances of doing so are diminishing with the time passing quickly. It would be a great calamity for democracy if it turned out that it is unable to prove itself in this age of great trial.

Notes

1. "The fragile 53", "The Economist", July 23, 2022, p. 62–63 (https://www.economist.com/finance-and-economics/2022/07/20/the-53-fragile-emerging-economies; access 8.08.2022).
2. The percentage of people aged 15 and over who can read and write is now 86.7. Until the 1940s, it did not exceed half of the world's population. It implies that still over a billion people cannot read or write. This applies in particular to girls and women, for whom this indicator is twice as high, i.e. as much as 26.7% can't read and write. This is one of the main causes of poverty and inequality.
3. "70% of 10-Year-Olds now in Learning Poverty, Unable to Read and Understand a Simple Text", The World Bank, Press Release, June 23, 2022 (https://www.worldbank.org/en/news/press-release/2022/06/23/70-of-10-year-olds-now-in-learning-poverty-unable-to-read-and-understand-a-simple-text; access 17.07.2022).
4. "Protecting child rights in a time of crises", UNICEF Annual Report 2021 (https://www.unicef.org/reports/unicef-annual-report-2021; access 17.07.2022).
5. "Climate change a bigger threat than war, Fiji tells security summit", "BBC News", June 12, 2022 (https://www.bbc.com/news/world-asia-61774473; access 6.07.2022).
6. "Investing in new fossil fuels is «moral and economic madness» – UN chief", "Energy Voice", April 4, 2022 (https://www.energyvoice.com/oilandgas/400595/investing-in-new-fossil-fuels-is-moral-and-economic-madness-un-chief/; access 2.08.2022).
7. Matt McGrath, "Climate change: «Madness» to turn to fossil fuels because of Ukraine war", "BBC World", March 21, 2022 (https://www.bbc.com/news/science-environment-60815547; access 6.07.2022).

19

Euro-Atlantic and Euro-Asian Mega-Systems Can Peacefully Compete and Cooperate

While Russia's international role is by no means doomed to be marginalized, although it will certainly be severely diminished, following its historical mistake, China has even more serious assets than before to further consolidate its position. One of the key elements of the evolution of future global geopolitical and economic mega-systems are the interrelationships of these large countries and their implications for global relations. There are many opinions on these issues, all the more reason to cite at least one coming this time from the East, from China.

According to an expert at the Beijing Centre for International Security and Strategy based at the renowned Tsinghua University, "In recent months speculation abounded that Beijing and Moscow's "unlimited" partnership—announced during Mr. Putin's visit to China in February for the Winter Olympics—might usher in a military alliance. But the war in Ukraine has inadvertently proved that Beijing and Moscow's rapprochement is not an alliance. China didn't provide military assistance to Russia. Instead, it provided humanitarian aid and money to Ukraine (…) and has pledged to continue to "play a constructive role". One reason behind the Sino-Russian non-alliance is that it allows a comfortable flexibility between two partners. And in spite of the fact that China and Russia both call for a multipolar world, a non-alliance suits them because they see such a world differently. (…) Russia sees itself as a victim of the existing international order. By contrast, China is the largest beneficiary of the rules and regulations of global commerce and finance made by the West after the Second World War. China has a huge stake in safeguarding the existing international order. This is why, despite ideological differences and even tensions sometimes, China has at least maintained robust economic ties with the West. Neither side wishes to sever them."[1] Another opportunity to strengthen bilateral mutual relations and coordinate policy on the world stage was the meeting of Chinese and Russian leaders during the summit of Shanghai Cooperation Organization, SCO, in Samarkand in mid-September of 2022.

When considering Russia, the many aspects of the complex political and economic consequences of its aggression are still not clear and entirely predictable, but it will certainly evolve in the post-Putin years in a very different direction from the astray it has gone. Not everyone necessarily thinks so. I have heard such a comment that even if Vladimir Putin and Alexei Navalny swapped places—and some think that they deserve such a permutation—nothing important would change in Russia anyway.

An influential British-American think tank suggests that "In the long term, one Western-bashing bloc (led by China and Russia) and one Western-leaning bloc (led by the US and the EU) will cement themselves into the geopolitical landscape and use economic and military levers to court countries that are not aligned with either side. We expect this competition for influence to expand rapidly beyond Asia and into Africa, the Middle East and Latin America."[2] Unfortunately, things have been going this way for some time now, and the reactions to the shock of Russia's invasion of Ukraine are catalyzing this further. This does not bode well. Instead of a confrontation along such a line, the Euro-Atlantic and Euro-Asian mega-systems can compete peacefully and cooperate without reaching for "military levers". Moreover, the strengthening of transnational economic, cultural and diplomatic levers may render the military ones useless. In both blocs, a key role should be played by the European Union, which, given its location, belongs to each of them and which does not have to take sides in the US–China disputes. It may be all to the good.

Just as Greta Thunberg said at the COP26 that it is never too late to do as much as we can in the fight for climate, so it must now be said that it is never too early to do as much as we can in the fight for peace. We have experience from the previous Cold War. It was absolutely too early to talk about peaceful coexistence and pragmatic cooperation during the Korean War in 1950–1953 or the Cuban Missile Crisis in 1962. It would also have been too early to talk about it (one can always think) during the "fraternal socialist aid" to Czechoslovakia in 1968. But as early as in the summer of 1975 it was possible to conclude the Conference on Security and Cooperation in Europe, CSCE with the "Final Act".[3]

The conference, held between 1973 and 1975, was a process of meetings held at various levels, substantive discussions, diplomatic disagreements, tough negotiations and, most importantly, compromise decisions resolving tensions between the East, led by the Soviet Union, and the West, led by the United States. During the CSCE, the Vietnam War also continued. The Americans fled Saigon only three months before the "Final Act" was agreed in Helsinki. It was signed by 35 signatories—all European except Maoist Albania, plus the US and Canada.

The CSCE applied to the whole of the Euro-Atlantic bloc and only to the northern part of the Euro-Asian bloc, on the Asian continent covering only its Russian part and the current post-Soviet republics. In China, which at that time did not matter much on the economic map of the world, it was only then that the reformist Deng Xiaoping took over the reins of power after the death of the orthodox Mao Zedong, while the so-called Third World, not only in Asia, was still getting back on its feet after liberating itself from colonialism. By the way, the support provided back then, in the 1950s, 1960s and 1970s, by the socialist states, especially the Soviet Union, and by China on a smaller scale, to the national liberation movements echoes today, as historical memory lasts, both about the colonial oppressors and those who helped in the struggle to eradicate the colonialism of the time. This factor still explains a lot today when it comes to, for example, the attitude of South Africa or Ethiopia toward Russia or Burkina Faso (Upper Volta in the colonial era) or Pakistan toward China.

It is too early now, someone will say, for a Helsinki-like conference. Just now, as if symbolically, Finlandia Hall—a beautiful architectural work by Alvar Aalto—in which the talks were held, is undergoing major refurbishment and even the symphony orchestra performing there has to play elsewhere; presenting not only Sibelius and Grieg but also Prokofiev and Shostakovich. Now, just now, it is the time for meetings at various levels, substantive discussions, diplomatic disagreements, tough negotiations and, most importantly, compromise decisions to relieve tension. There is no need to wait because it will not get any easier later on. I wonder when and where a similar conference to the Helsinki one half a century ago will be held? Maybe again at Finlandia Hall, once this edifice is refurbished…

Notes

1. Zhou Bo, "The war in Ukraine…", *op. cit*.
2. "What does the Ukraine crisis mean for the US?", The Economist Intelligence Unit, April 12, 2022 (https://www.eiu.com/n/what-does-the-ukraine-crisis-mean-for-the-us/; access 26.05.2022).
3. The "Final Act" covered four so-called baskets of cases. The first basket included European security issues, together with the principles of state-to-state relations and confidence-building measures. The second basket covered problems of economic, scientific and technical cooperation and environmental protection. The third basket referred to human rights and humanitarian cooperation in other areas. The fourth basket dealt with the mode of continuation of the work of the CSCE.

20

Something Far Worse Than the Seven Plagues of the Bible

In these difficult times, there is little good news. According to some, there is a war for peace, according to others, there is war and peace. Probably a Russian translation of this book would appear under the title "Special Military Operation and Peace". One gets the impression that someone irresponsible (more often) or some bad luck (less often) has opened a twenty-first-century Pandora's box and all sorts of nasty things are now crawling out of it: militarism and wars, terrorism and crime, pandemics and pestilences, hot climate and weather anomalies, neoliberalism and new authoritarianism, populism and new nationalism, poverty and hunger, uncontrolled migration and ethnic conflicts, inflation and shortages, recession and crises. These twenty plagues are not only much more but they are also something far worse than the seven plagues of the Bible.

Between 2020 and 2021, nine out of ten countries fell in the rankings of the Human Development Index. The HDI, estimated by the United Nations Development Program, UNDP, decreased to 0.732. The causes of this collapse are climate change, the COVID-19 pandemic and the war in Ukraine. 2022 is even gloomier in this respect. The deterioration of the situation in most of the 191 countries analyzed by UNDP, especially in terms of life expectancy, which weighs one-third on HDI values, reversed the 30-year upward trend, bringing human development back to the 2017 level.

Someone may also have the impression that the world, or more precisely the people who inhabit it, seem to have got lost in the jungle of problems that surround them and seem to be less aware of the seriousness of the situation.

We have become accustomed to living in peace for three generations now. The shocking war in Ukraine has only slightly shaken the prevailing tranquility—and by no means worldwide—as time has done its work. There is hardly anyone among us any more who experienced the atrocities of the Second World War. Perhaps this is why it is so easy for bellicose politicians to push and impose a wasteful arms race on their societies because this is supposed to save us from some kind of war as if peace movements and at least partial disarmament could not do so. The world is in a trap and this is why it needs not some idealistic pacifists to whom no one listens, but pragmatic peace activists of the kind that were plenty during that First Cold War.

Populism is developing in response to the great disappointment brought about by neoliberalism, but—once again—the enemy of our enemy does not make him our friend. Now we have not just two enemies: neoliberalism and populism. There are more of these foes because, in response to the failure of liberal democracy to address social and environmental problems, which require strong social cohesion, deep divisions and antagonistic fractures in societies have occurred. Instead of compactness and the ability to make an organized team effort to solve common problems, these fractures degenerate societies into two hostile factions, almost into warring tribes, of which the best, or rather worst, examples are the supporters of Republicans and Democrats in the United States.

In response to the lack of skills to carry out compromising negotiations and reconcile the conflicting interests occurring in the international arena in a conciliatory manner, conflict-triggering situations become conflict situations. In turn, in response to them, the Second Cold War was triggered, escalating into a wasteful arms race and harmful militarism.

It is bad, it will get even worse. It is going to get worse, but it does not have to get much worse, because basically all the problems troubling humanity are solvable. Solvable, but they are not being solved. And if they are not being solved, it may be that they will not be solved. To avoid this, to find a way out of the trap in which this world of ours is entangled, it is necessary to have a rational vision of its peaceful functioning and sustainable development, not illusions—coming from the right or left side, rarely deriving from common sense.

It is necessary to have political strategies that take into account the values guiding the various societies and the different, sometimes considerably, interests of the various states. It is necessary to have economic strategies that blend one's socio-economic development into irreversible globalization, which needs to be made more inclusive in the process of international alignment and re-institutionalization. It is necessary to have political leaders who look ahead beyond their national backyards and beyond the next elections and who can take a courageous and pragmatic approach to dealing with the difficult reality.

In addition to the above, a deep understanding of what is happening and why is needed. It is essential to properly set immediate and especially long-term economic, social and environmental policy goals. Determination and the ability to coordinate policies at supranational levels are indispensable. Peace is needed, even if cold, but not cold war and armament race. Finally, a proper theory of integrated development is necessary, on which a rational and progressive policy could be based. This is the purpose of a new pragmatism—a framework of a theoretical concept within the postulative current of economic science based on the desire for a good economy that meets the challenges of the present day.

The new pragmatism is a heterodox paradigmatic profile of economic theory created as a response to the challenges of civilization and the transformations of economic systems. An essential part of the paradigm shift in economics is to move away from the dictates of profit maximization and production growth as the goal of economic activity and to formulate it anew, taking into account the imperative of subordinating the short-term interests of private capital to the long-term interests of the public. An important principle governing the economy of the future should be moderation, i.e. the conscious adjustment of the size of human, material and financial flows and stocks to the requirement of maintaining a long-term dynamic equilibrium.

It should be reiterated here that under the new pragmatism, economics is seen as a science, which is:

1. Descriptive—the analysis and description of the state of affairs constitute a foundation for the diagnosis and a starting point for further considerations.
2. Explanatory—the interpretation of the observed phenomena and processes facilitates the understanding of why they manifest themselves and occur as they do and not otherwise.
3. Evaluative—the evaluation of alternative *ex post* situations and expected *ex ante* results forces us to seek answers to the question of whether it could have been better and whether it can be better in the future.
4. Normative—postulating directions and methods of change for the better, following the judgement as to what appears to be better and why.
5. Comprehensive—observing the whole of economic relations in the broadest sense, without succumbing to reductionism and attempting to build comprehensive theories from fragmentary research results.

6. Eclectic—connecting lines of analysis and synthesis of various economic schools: from classical economics through neo-Keynesian, institutional and behavioral economics to development economics and political economy, as well as microeconomics with macroeconomics and global economics.
7. Contextual—in which the analyses and syntheses are not detached from reality, in models of 'pure' economics, but refer to specific, dynamic, and variable complex circumstances, conditions, constraints, and opportunities.
8. Multidisciplinary—in which the analysis of economic reality takes into account the findings and methods of other social science disciplines, primarily philosophy, sociology, psychology, law, political science, and anthropology, as well as history and geography.
9. Comparative—in which the comparison of economic, cultural, political, geographical, and environmental realities in time and space is treated as a basic research method. The scientific process largely consists of comparing and drawing conclusions based on the comparisons made.

Descriptively, new pragmatism explains the historical development process, highlighting not only the importance of the individual drivers but also their co-occurrence (coincidence). Normatively, new pragmatism indicates prosperity in its broadest sense as an objective of economic activity. Pursuing it requires:

- economically sustainable development, i.e. relating to commodity and capital markets, investment and finance markets, as well as the workforce,
- socially sustainable development, i.e. relating to a distribution of income that is accepted by the population as being both fair and conducive to the accumulation of capital, with adequate access to public services,
- environmentally and spatially sustainable development, i.e. relating to the maintenance of appropriate relations between human business activity and nature, both on an ongoing basis and in a forward-looking manner. The spatial aspect is also important, as without proper consideration of it, there is no natural, architectural, or urban harmony.

Unfortunately, we have lived to see such times during which hardly anyone wants to discuss the search for a new paradigm of economy or debate a modern strategy of socio-economic development. No time to grieve for roses when the forests are burning. And they burn—literally and figuratively. There are many cautions, especially regarding the war in Ukraine, that the fire may be much greater than what we are already experiencing. "Although disastrous escalation may be avoided, the warring parties' ability to manage that danger is far from certain. The risk of it is substantially greater than the conventional wisdom holds. And given that the consequences of escalation could include a major war in Europe and possibly even nuclear annihilation, there is good reason for extra concern."[1] I trust that this book brings a little bit of unconventional wisdom and may contribute to so much-needed extra concern.

Something good, however, is also happening. From the various small things that bring joy to each of us, to the milestones of humanity that we owe to the scientific and technological progress, mentioned at the beginning of these reflections among the seven critical megatrends. While millions of people are suffering from human-induced humanitarian crises, the James Webb Space Telescope, JWST, is voyaging through the skies. Thanks to its superb technology, its apparatus is able to photograph celestial objects 13.3 billion light years away—objects that emitted their light shortly after the Big Bang, which created this challenging universe of ours. What is fascinating is that much of what we see thanks to the JWST has not existed for a long time, sometimes for billions of years. There can be a star that has stopped shining, that is no longer there, but we still see it. If the Sun were to go out, it would shine on us for another eight minutes, because that is how long its luminous rays flash to the Earth. At the same time, we cannot see the mass of celestial bodies that exist and emit light but are so far away from us that it has not yet had time to reach the Earth.

The same, albeit on a very different time scale, is happening in the universe of contemporary environmental, political and socio-economic issues. While the JWST measures time in thousands, millions and billions of light years, we measure it in hours, days, quarters, years, decades and centuries. We still see and engage in fierce arguments concerning some issues, although they are no longer there because they have passed. Others are there, by all means, but we do not see them yet. The intention of my reflections I am sharing here is not to waste precious time dwelling too much on the issues of yesterday, but to focus on the challenges of tomorrow. And let the Earth continue to revolve in peace, as Okudzhava wants it to in his "Prayer"[2]:

While yet the Earth is revolving,
While yet the daylight is broad,
Lord, pray, give everyone.
Whatever they have in want:
Give the wise one more brilliance,
The coward a horse to flee,

Give the happy some money…
And don't forget about me.

In October 2022, it was still revolving…

Notes

1. John J. Mearsheimer, *op. cit.*
2. Bulat Okudzhava, "Molitva" (1963), "TextyPesen.com (https://textypesen.com/bulat-okudzava/molitva/; access 11.07.2022). English translation according to "Lyrics Translate" (https://lyricstranslate.com/en/prayer-francois-villon-prayer-francois-villon.html; access 17.09.2022).

Bibliography

Åslund A (2019) Russia's crony capitalism: the path from market economy to kleptocracy. Yale University Press, New Haven

Belton C (2020) Putin's people: how the KGB took back Russia and then took on the West. Farrar, Straus and Giroux, New York

Bo Z (2022) The war in Ukraine will accelerate the geopolitical shift from West to East. The Economist. https://www.economist.com/by-invitation/2022/05/14/senior-colonel-zhou-bo-says-the-war-in-ukraine-will-accelerate-the-geopolitical-shift-from-west-to-east. Access 13 May 2022

Bullough O (2022) Butler to the world: how Britain become the servant of oligarchs, tax dodgers, kleptocrats and criminals. Profile Books, London

Brzezinski Z (2007) Second chance: three presidents and the crisis of American superpower. Basic Books, New York, pp 64

Chotiner I (2022) Why John Mearsheimer Blames the U.S. for the crisis in Ukraine, The New Yorker. https://www.newyorker.com/news/q-and-a/why-john-mearsheimer-blames-the-us-for-the-crisis-in-ukraine. Access 08 March 2022

Dawisha K (2014) Putin's kleptocracy: who owns Russia? Simon and Shuster, New York, London

Frankopan P (2012) The first crusade: the call from the east. The Belknap Press for Harvard University Press, Cambridge, Massachusetts and London

Gardner F (2022a) Tighter export controls on electronics could hamper Russia's war effort—report. BBC News. https://www.bbc.com/news/world-europe-62464459. Access 8 August 2022

Gardner F (2022b) NATO summit: five challenges for the military alliance. BBC News. June 28. https://www.bbc.com/news/world-61924778. Access 28 June 2022

Grytsenko A (2022) Hybrid system peace-war» as a modern form of the changing world order. In: Grytsenko A, Kidiryuz M (eds) Proceeding book: 2. international symposium on war studies, 20–21 May 2022, Ankara, pp 67–73. https://www.izdas.org/_files/ugd/262ebf_c81b0674b9774454af80bdb40bc70421.pdf. Access 12 July 2022

Hamadeh N, Van Rompey C, Metreau E, Eapen SG (2022) New World Bank country classifications by income level: 2022–2023. The World Bank, Washington, DC. https://blogs.worldbank.org/opendata/new-world-bank-country-classifications-income-level-2022-2023. Access 26 August 2022

Hufbauer C, Schott JJ, Elliott KA, Oegg B (2021) Economic sanctions reconsidered. Peterson Institute for International Relations, Washington, DC

Jackson J (2022) Madeleine Albright saying Iraqi Kids deaths worth it resurfaces. Newsweek. https://www.newsweek.com/watch-madeleine-albright-saying-iraqi-kids-deaths-worth-it-resurfaces-1691193. Access 3 July 2022

Kolodko GW (2008) Truth, errors, and lies: politics and economics in a volatile world. Columbia University Press, New York, p 238

Kolodko GW (2022) Political economy of new pragmatism: implications of irreversible globalization. Springer, Cham

Kolodko GW (2022) Blog. Truth, errors, and lies: politics and economics in a volatile world, post 2506, November 10, 2014 . https://www.wedrujacyswiat.pl/blog/kolodko/. Access 15 July 2022

Kissinger H (2022) These are the main geopolitical challenges facing the world right now. World Econ Forum Ann Meet. https://www.weforum.org/agenda/2022/05/kissinger-these-are-the-main-geopolitical-challenges-facing-the-world-right-now/. Access 31 July 2022

Kahneman D (2011) Thinking, fast and slow. Farrar, Strauss and Giroux, New York

Kissinger HA (2022) To settle the Ukraine crisis, start at the end. The Washington Post. https://www.washingtonpost.com/opinions/henry-kissinger-to-settle-the-ukraine-crisis-start-at-the-end/2014/03/05/46dad868-a496-11e3-8466-d34c451760b9_story.html. Access 08 March 2022

Knell Y, Maishman E (2022) Israel-Gaza: death toll rises as Israel targets militants. BBC News. https://www.bbc.com/news/world-middle-east-62445951. Access 6 August 2022

Kolodko GW, McMahon WW (1987) Stagflation and shortageflation: a comparative approach. Kyklos 40(2):176–197

Kolodko GW (2018) Socialism, capitalism, or Chinism? Communist Post-Communist Stud 51(4):285–298

Kolodko GW (2021) Shortageflation 3.0: war economy—state socialism—pandemic crisis. Acta Oeconomica 13–34

Khadka NS (2022) Ukraine calls for Nepal to ban Russian climbers from Himalayas. BBC News. https://www.bbc.com/news/world-asia-60915320. Access 30 March 2022

Lovell J (2020) Maoism: a global history. Vintage Books, New York, p 16

Maçães B (2020) Belt and road: a Chinese world order. Hurts, London

McGrath M (2022a) Climate change: key UN finding widely misinterpreted. BBC News. https://www.bbc.com/news/science-environment-61110406. Access 16 April 2022

McGrath M (2022b) Climate change: "Madness" to turn to fossil fuels because of Ukraine war. BBC World. https://www.bbc.com/news/science-environment-60815547. Access 6 July 2022

Mearsheimer J (2022a) Why the West is principally responsible for the Ukrainian crisis. The Economist. https://www.economist.com/by-invitation/2022a/03/11/john-mearsheimer-on-why-the-west-is-principally-responsible-for-the-ukrainian-crisis. Access 17 March 2022

Mearsheimer JJ (2022b) Playing with fire in Ukraine. The underappreciated risks of catastrophic escalation. Foreign Aff. https://natyliesbaldwin.com/2022b/08/john-mearsheimer-playing-with-fire-in-ukraine/. Access 29 August 2022

Molloy D (2022) Taiwan: Nancy Pelosi trip labelled as extremely dangerous by Beijing. BBC News. https://www.bbc.com/news/world-asia-62398029. Access 3 August 2022

Moloney M (2022) United States to appoint first Arctic Ambassador. BBC News. https://www.bbc.com/news/world-us-canada-62699129. Access 27 August 2022

Mulder N (2022) Russia's economic isolation will have dramatic repercussions for the world economy. The Economist. https://www.economist.com/by-invitation/2022/03/04/nicholas-mulder-who-studies-sanctions-declares-a-watershed-moment-in-global-economic-history. Access 3 March 2022

Murphy M (2022) Ukraine war: US wants to see a weakened Russia. BBC News. https://www.bbc.com/news/world-europe-61214176. Access 1 July 2022

Novokmet F, Piketty T, Zucman G (2017) From soviets to oligarchs: inequality and property in Russia, 1905–2016. In: NBER working paper No. 23712, National Bureau of Economic Research, Cambridge, MA

Okudzhava B (1963) Molitva. TextyPesen.com. https://textypesen.com/bulat-okudzava/molitva/. Access 11 July 2022. English translation according to "Lyrics Translate". https://lyricstranslate.com/en/prayer-francois-villon-prayer-francois-villon.html. Access 17 September 2022

Peter L (2022) Ukraine conflict: Ban Russian visitors, Zelensky urges West. BBC News. https://www.bbc.com/news/world-europe-62480087. Access 9 August 2022

Rhodes B (2022) After the fall: the rise of authoritarianism in the world we've made. Random House, New York

Rodrik D (2022) Getting productivism right, Project Syndicate. The World's Opinion Page. https://www.project-syndicate.org/commentary/will-productivism-supersede-neoliberalism-by-dani-rodrik-2022-08?utm_source=twitter&utm_medium=organic-social&utm_campaign=page-posts-aug22&utm_post-type=link&utm_format=16:9&utm_creative=link-image&utm_post-date=2022-08-08. Access 10 August 2022

Sater D (1998) The rise of the Russian criminal state. Jamestown Foundation. Washington, D.C.

Snyder T (2022) We should say it. Russia Is Fascist. The New York Times. https://www.nytimes.com/2022/05/19/opinion/russia-fascism-ukraine-putin.html. Access 16 August 2022

Wiatr JJ (ed) (2019) New authoritarianism: challenges to democracy in the 21st century. Verlag Barbara Budrich, Opladen—Berlin—Toronto, pp 173–174

Wedel JR (1998a) Collision and collusion: the strange case of western aid to Eastern Europe 1989–1998. St. Martin's Press, New York

Wedel JR (1998b) The Harvard boys do Russia. The Nation, pp 11–16

Wiatr JJ (2021) Political leadership: between democracy and authoritarianism. Barbara Budrich Publishers, Opladen—Berlin—Toronto, p 162

York G (2022) Tigray war has seen up to half a million dead from violence and starvation, say researchers. The Globe and Mail. https://www.theglobeandmail.com/world/article-tigray-war-has-seen-up-to-half-a-million-dead-from-violence-and/. Access 20 March 2022

Index

Aalto, Alvar 147
Abkhazia 102
Afghanistan 11, 83
Africa
   sub-Saharan 82
African-Americans 126
Albania 50, 98, 147
Al-Bashir, Omar 50
Albright, Madeleine 82
Algeria 15, 20, 114, 141, 142
Algiers 141
Al-Nakhala, Ziyad 110
Al-Qaeda 52
Alternative scenarios for future
   changes 7
America
   Latin 139, 146
   Southern 89
Americans 5, 7, 12–14, 22, 23, 25,
   33, 36, 37, 39, 40, 42, 43, 51,
   56, 58, 65, 67, 87, 89, 99,
   102–104, 107, 109, 113, 115,
   119, 126–128, 133, 147
Amnesty International 38, 39
Anarchization 106, 125
Angola 52, 92, 128, 141, 142
Angolan People's Liberation
   Movement, MPLA 128
Ankara 25
Anti-American 14
Anti-Chinese 88
Anti-German 33
Anti-Russian
   restrictions 61, 76, 129
   sanctions 91, 103
   sentiment 13
Apartheid in South Africa 50
AR-15 rifle 126
Arab Emirates 56, 141
Arab Spring 129
ARAMCO 141
Arctic 106, 107, 142
Argentina 92
Armed Forces of the Russian
   Federation 41, 47
Armenia 20
Arms export 107, 114
Arms race 116, 118–120, 124, 138,
   144, 150

Arms spiral 110
AS-90 howitzers 113
ASEAN 88
Asia
  Central 21, 69
Assamese 24
Atlantic 14, 45, 104, 106, 146
Atlantic Council 57
Austin, Lloyd 39, 100
Australia 88, 91, 108, 114, 141
Austria 33, 55, 124
Authoritarian
  countries 56
  regime 68, 125, 123, 129, 130
  system 68, 130
Authoritarianism
  model 69
  new 68, 69, 71, 81, 128, 149
  old 68
Azerbaijan 20

Bachelet, Michelle 42
Baikal 60
Bali 134
Balkan wars 50
Baltic 36, 100, 141
Baltic countries 36
Bangladesh 83, 106, 114, 128
Barriers, protectionist 88
Baskets of cases 148
Basques 25
Bavaria 76
BBC
  World News 114
Behavioral economics 79, 152
Beijing 22, 23, 26, 68, 98, 106, 118, 119, 145
Belarus 30, 81, 110, 130
Belgium 115, 124, 139
Belt and Road Initiative (BRI) 98, 104, 105
Benin 92

Berlin
  wall 6
  west 21
Biden, Joe 13, 22, 26, 39, 42, 49, 87, 88, 107, 133, 143
Big Bang 153
Birobidzhan 60
Black Sea 65, 95
Blitzkrieg 15, 109
BMW 67
Bolivia 20
Bolshoi theatre 60
Boric, Gabriel 127
Botswana 92
BrahMos missile 20
Brain drain 97
Brainwashing 8
Braveheart 113
Brazil 78, 89, 91, 92, 108, 127, 128
Breakthrough in Poland in 1989 50
Brennan Center for Justice 126
British 7, 16, 25, 36, 37, 39, 42, 43, 50, 59, 103, 110, 113, 129, 134, 146
Brunei 20, 88, 91, 92
Brussels 12, 33, 66
Brzezinski, Zbigniew 58, 63, 101
Bucharest 13
Budget deficit 43, 93, 118, 133
Bulgaria 36, 50, 61
Bulletin of the Atomic Scientists 22, 26
Burkina Faso 92, 147

California 76, 126
Callamard, Agnès 38
Cambodia 22, 88, 105
Cambridge Bay 106, 142
Canada 61, 89, 106, 147
Cape Verde 92
Caracas 51
Carbon dioxide emissions

net greenhouse gas emissions 124
Castillo, Pedro 127
Catalans 25
Catherine II the Great 32
CBS 82
Center for International Security and Strategy 145
Central African Republic 52
Central banks 31, 32, 56, 73, 74, 77, 126
Chad 83
Chagos archipelago 25
Chauvinism 25
Chihuahua 14
Chile 15, 20, 92, 106, 108, 125, 127
China 3, 14, 20–25, 27, 36, 50, 52, 56, 57, 61, 68, 77, 78, 88–91, 98–100, 102–107, 109, 113, 114, 116, 118, 120, 134, 136, 140, 145–147
Chinese people 68
Chinism 105, 106, 110
CIA 58
Ciudad de Juarez 14
Ciudad de Mexico 14
Climate
  catastrophe of, overheating 124
  change 1, 23, 97, 120, 124, 130, 134–136, 140, 144, 149
  emergency 143
  overheating 124, 133
  policy 74, 134
  transition 136
  warming 3, 106, 125, 134, 144
Climate crusade 23
Climate emergency 143
CNN 55, 115
Coahuila 14
Coffee Star 67
Cold War
  atmosphere of 113
  current 21, 106, 139
  First 55, 103, 105, 115, 150

New 104
previous 23, 97
Second 3, 101, 103, 107, 108, 144, 150
Cold war amok 113
Colombia 127, 130
Colonialism
  French 15
  legacy of 20
  Portuguese 128
  struggle to eradicate 147
Combined Drought Indicator (CDI) 123
Common Market of the South, Mercosur 92
Conference on Security and Cooperation in Europe (CSCE) 146–148
Congo
  Democratic Republic of 52, 92
Conservative-nationalist media 32
Conservative orientation 32
Constitutional Court
  of Malawi 127
  of Ukraine 15, 17
Consumer Price Index (CPI) 75, 120
Consumer spending 75
COP26 97, 124, 146
COP27 124, 134
Corruption
  and inefficient mechanisms of limited democracy 96
  Perception 96
  Russian 58
Corsicans 25
Côte d'Ivoire 52, 92
Coup 41, 128
COVID-19 6, 62, 74, 79, 138, 149
COVID-19 coronavirus pandemic 97
Crimea 12, 40, 41, 47, 96, 102
Crimea annexation 12, 104
Croatia 61

Cross-Border Interbank Payment
    System (CIPS) 57
Cuba 50, 51
Cursed soldiers"@"Cursed soldiers"
    37
Czechoslovakia 146
Czech Republic 36, 61, 77, 124

Daily income 76, 93, 94
Debt relief process 98
Decree of the President of the
    Russian Federation 47
Deficit
    budget 43, 93, 118, 133
    trade 61
Demilitarization of Ukraine 8
Democracy
    American 37, 126, 128
    beauties of 101
    direct 125
    full 125
    hybrid 96
    liberal 3, 14, 41, 67, 127, 150
    limited 96
    model of 129
    progress of 129
    relative 129
    strong 126
    true 14, 127
    vibrant 22
Denazification of Ukraine 8, 37
Deng Xiaoping 21, 147
Denmark 55, 77, 106
Deoligarchization 96, 98
Deutsche Welle 55
Diaoyu 21
Diego Garcia 25
Dnipro 15
Dnipropetrovsk 15
Dolce & Gabbana 65
Dollar, confidence in 56
Donbas 1, 7, 8, 67, 96

Dongfeng ballistic missiles 23
Doomsday Clock 22, 26, 42
Dostoevsky, Fyodor 8
Draghi, Mario 45
Drone
    drone-carried MAM-L missiles
        113
Drought 75, 123, 124
Duda, Andrzej 43
Dutch Front Month Futures 75

EagleEye 107
East China Sea 21
Economic Community of West
    African States 92
Economic misery
    index 77
    rate 78
Economic sanctions 50, 52, 59, 142
Economic strategies 150
Economies, emancipating 104, 108,
    109
"Economist" 6, 37, 65, 66, 70, 74,
    79, 89, 90, 93, 96, 101, 114,
    128
Economist Intelligence Unit 148
Economy
    American 130
    Chinese 87, 99
    deoligarchization of 96
    devastated 98
    export-oriented 31
    global 26, 76, 139, 152
    globalized 61, 91
    good 151
    important principle governing
        151
    low carbon 136
    market 62, 98, 127
    national 79, 90, 91
    natural farming 94
    new paradigm of 152

Russia's 81, 91
War 80
world 53, 90
ECOWAS, Economic Community of West African States 92
Ecuador 89, 93, 128
Egypt 50, 91, 114, 134
Ekonomichna Teoriya 70
Ekonomika Ukrainy 70
Elections
   2022 congressional 89
   annulled 127
   basically free (if not always fair) 68
   democratic 128
   parliamentary 33, 128
Emancipating economies 103, 108, 109
Emancipating societies 108, 109
Embargo
   limiting the sale of oil and gas from Russia on world markets 61
   on Mussolini's fascist Italy 50
   partial or full 67
   preventing Russia from using SWIFT 57
Emerging markets 108
Emigration
   economic 83
   hastened 95
   potential 140
Employment agency EWL 100
Energy prices
   growth of 61
   rising 75
Energy transition 31, 97, 135, 141, 142
Equilibrium, long-term dynamic 151
Erdoğan, Recep 107
Eritrea 52, 110
Ermath, Fritz M. 58
ERM II 32
Estonia 56, 60, 91, 98, 100
Eswatini 92
Ethiopia 50, 52, 83, 93, 136, 147
EU-China cooperation 100
Eurasia 142
Euro-Atlantic and Euro-Asian mega-systems 145
Eurobonds 57
Europe
   Central 35, 99
   Eastern 1, 35, 36, 63, 99
   Western 69, 95, 105, 142
European Charter for Regional and Minority Languages 17
European Commission 42, 61, 62, 97, 130
European Fund for Reconstruction of Ukraine (EFRU) 97, 99
European Investment Bank (EIB) 94
Europeans 30–33, 36, 43, 55, 61, 69, 83, 97, 98, 103, 115, 116, 119, 123, 147
European security 116, 148
European Union (EU) 14, 29, 33, 56, 60, 74, 89, 96–98, 103, 116, 123, 134, 143, 146
Eurostat 142
Eurozone 61

"Facts" TVN 115
Far North 106
Fascism, criteria of 37
Federal Republic of Germany 29
Federation of American Scientists 25
Fiji 91, 140
Filibuster 126
Financial and economic crisis 6
Financial compensation from Germany 30, 31
Financial restrictions 57
Finland
   hall 147
Finlandization 115

Fiscalism 118
Fiscal policy 77, 78, 127
Florida 58, 127
Food and Agriculture Organization (FAO) 37
Foreign debt reduction 97
Foreign exchange reserves 56
Format 16+1 100
Format 17+1 100
Foundation for Urban Projects 40
Fox News 115
France 25, 52, 60, 61, 103, 110, 114, 124, 139, 141, 142
Frederick William II 32
French Riviera 57
Fujimori, Keiko 127
Future
  costs of combating global Warming 133
  economy of 151
  evolution of future global geopolitical and economic mega-systems 145
  inevitable 7
  possible 7

G7 61, 94, 104
G20 139
Gambia 92
Gartner, consultancy 62
Gaza 110
Gazeta Polska Codziennie 115
Gazeta Wyborcza 115
Gazprom 63
Georgia 14, 102, 126
Gergiev, Valery 69
German Marshall Fund (GMF) 94
Germanophobia 31
Germany 21, 29–31, 33, 34, 50, 59–61, 94, 97, 103, 104, 110, 114, 119, 124, 139, 141, 142

Gerrymandering (manipulation of electoral district boundaries) 126
Ghana 92
Ghebreyesus, Tedros Adhanom 83
Gibraltar 63
Glapiński, Adam 31, 34
Glasgow 97, 124
Global Drought Observatory (GDO) 123
Globalization
  desirable 90
  fragile 89
  irreversible 2, 3, 108, 150
  non-inclusive 3
  political 105
Global warming
  combat 97, 133, 135, 138
  fight against 133, 142, 144
  life-threatening 124
Gogol, Nikolai 69
Golan Heights 24
Gold 57
Greece 27, 50, 77, 98
Greenland 106
Grieg, Edvard 147
Gross Domestic Product (GDP) 26, 134
Gross National Income (GNI) 108
Gross world product 134, 138
Guerra del Pacífico 20
Guinea
  Bissau 52, 92
Guterres, António 41, 42, 142

Habsburgs 33
Haiti 52, 106
Hamas 110
Harris, Kamala 27
Helsinki 15, 147
Hermitage 60

High Mobility Artillery Rocket
    System (HIMARS) 40
History
    alternative 11
    "the end of" 103
Household budget surveys 76
Hryvnia 94, 95, 99
Human Development Index (HDI)
    149
Humanitarian
    aid 83, 84, 97, 145
    costs 38
    crisis 82, 93, 96, 153
    law 38, 39
Hungary 60, 61, 108, 124, 128, 143
Hybrid
    democracy 96
    "peace-war" system 66
    political and economic system
        105

Iceland 106
Imperialism 14
India 20, 24, 25, 50, 56, 61, 91,
    105, 107, 108, 114, 123, 136
Indian Air Force 20
Indian Ocean 25
Indian subcontinent 20
Indoctrination centers 115
Indonesia 15, 60, 88, 91, 105, 108,
    134
Indo-Pacific Economic Framework
    for Prosperity (IPEF) 87, 88
Inflation 31, 43, 59, 61, 62, 73–80,
    95, 97, 115, 133, 149
Inflation rate 59, 74, 75, 77, 78
Inflation Reduction Act, IRA 133
Inflation versus unemployment,
    dilemma of 78
Influence game 101
Interest rates 77, 78, 98, 118, 139

International Energy Agency (IEA)
    60, 135
International food trade 38
International liquidity 57
International Monetary Fund (IMF)
    26, 93, 98
International Panel on Climate
    Change (IPCC) 124
International system of coordinated
    political cooperation 13
Invasion
    Russia of Ukraine 11, 15, 19, 22,
        26, 31, 59, 74, 82, 93, 115,
        146
    US of Iraq 104
Investment in underdeveloped
    countries 104
Iran 20, 21, 49–52, 107, 113
Iraq 24, 52, 82, 129
Ireland 124
Irian Jaya 24
Irkutsk 60
ISIL (Daish) 52
Israel 25, 26, 107, 110, 118
Israeli-Palestinian conflict 66, 110
Issa 24
Italy 50, 61, 119, 124, 139, 141,
    142

Jamestown Foundation 58, 63
James Webb Space Telescope
    (JWST) 153
Japan 19, 21, 50, 61, 88, 89, 91,
    108, 116, 139, 141
Jaruzelski, Wojciech 51
Javelins cumulative charge anti-tank
    armament 113
Johnnie Walker 65
Johnson, Boris 16, 39, 42, 45
Jordan 129
JP Morgan bank 63

Kaczyński Jarosław 45, 120
Kaliningrad 65
Kallas, Kaja 55
Kamchatka 60
Kandinsky, Wassily 8
Kansai 76
Karakalpakstan 102
Kashmir 20
Kashubia 15
Kautiyla 109
Kazakhstan 102
Kekkonen, Urho 115
Kenya 60, 127, 128
Keynes, John Maynard 6
Khabarovsk 60
Khamenei, Ali 107
Khmer Rouge 105
Kiev 39
Kissinger, Henry 12, 66, 71
Klympush-Tsintsadze, Ivanna 43
Kolodko, Grzegorz W. 3, 63, 110
Kommersant 115
Korea
   North 26, 50–52, 110, 119
   South 19, 88, 89, 91, 108, 114
Korean Peninsula 44
Kosovars 25
Kosovo
   independence 27
Kremlin
   autocratic or hostile inclinations
     to other countries 59
   brainwashing 8
   delusions 15
   propaganda 40, 115
   ruler 22
Kurds 24, 25

Lady Macbeth 69
Laos 88
Lapid, Yair 110
Latinos 126
Latvia 66, 98, 100
Lavrov, Sergei 14, 36
Law and Justice, PiS 45, 74
League of Nations 50
Lebanon 52, 61
Lena 60
Lesotho 92
Leyen, Ursula, von der 42
Liberia 52, 92
Libya 52, 129
Lingua franca 15
Liquefied Natural Gas (LNG) 141
Lithuania 30, 81, 98, 100
Litoral 20
Loch Ness 6
London 12, 57, 62, 66
London Club 98
Lower Silesia 15
Low-income countries 75, 108, 139, 140
Lugano 94
Lugansk
   region 67
Lula da Silva, Inácio 127
Luxembourg 124, 130
Lviv 41

M777 howitzers 113
Macron, Emmanuel 12, 45
Madagascar 92
Madrid 118
Madrid summit 2022 118
Maduro, Nicolás 116
Maidan 12, 43, 104
Make America Great Again! 128
Malawi 92
Malayan Emergency 105
Malaysia 20, 88, 91, 92
Mali 52
Manipulation of public opinion 114
Maoism 105, 106

Mao Zedong 105, 147
Mariinsky Theatre 60
Marin, Sanna 116
Mariupol 96
Market economy 62, 79, 98, 127
Matamoros 14
Matra power plant 143
Mauritius 92
McDonald's 67, 109
Mearsheimer, John J. 12–14, 16, 39, 40, 154
Medvedev, Dmitry 36, 41, 46, 47
Mega-systems
    Euro-Asian 145, 146
    Euro-Atlantic 145, 146
    geopolitical and global 145
Mercosur (Spanish: Mercado Común del Sur) 92
Meritocracy 105, 129
Metropolitan Opera 69
Mexico 92, 96, 108, 130
Middle East 21, 44, 51, 56, 66, 82, 99, 104, 131, 146
Militarism 119, 149, 150
Military budget 118, 119, 137
Military-industrial complex 110
Minister of finance 57, 98, 101
Minority languages 15
Moderation 151
Moldova 36, 102, 124
Monetary policy 32, 74, 77, 78
Monroe Doctrine 14
Montenegro 98
Morocco 20, 25, 89, 129
Moscow 11–13, 22, 35, 39, 40, 55, 59, 60, 66, 98, 106, 110, 145
Mozambique 76, 92, 130
Mugabe, Robert 50, 105
Museveni, Yoweri 128
Mussolini, Benito 50
Myanmar 83, 88

N
Nagorno-Karabakh 20
Namibia 92
Nation 25, 30, 69, 81
National Academy of Science of Ukraine 70
National Bank of Poland (NBP) 32, 34, 74, 75, 80
National Chengchi University in Taipei 24
National liberation movements 147
NATO
    Finland's accession to NATO 116
    Scandinavian countries' accession to 25
NATO's further expansion to the East 12
NATO's political cohesion 33
Natural gas 56, 75, 141
Navalny, Alexei 146
Neoliberalism
    disappointing 127
    pathologies 58
Nepal 105
Netherlands 59, 124
Netrebko, Anna 69
New nationalism 32, 106, 149
New pragmatism 2, 151, 152
New Silk Road 98
New York Post 115
New York Times 37, 115
New Zealand 88, 91, 108
Next Generation Light Anti-Tank Weapon (NLAW) 113
Niger 92, 96, 139
Nigeria 92, 136
Nogales 14
Nord Stream 1 142
Nord Stream 2 141
North Atlantic 104
North Atlantic and Arctic Treaty Organization (NAATO) 106
Norway 55, 97, 106, 139, 141
Nuclear

alarm 124
Armageddon 40, 84
energy 143
warheads 20, 25
weapons 20, 22, 49, 84
Nuevo Laredo 14
Nunavut 106

Occupation of Arab lands, by Israel 44
Oil
  embargo limiting the sale of 61
  imported via pipelines to
    European Union countries 61
  Russian 60
  Vegetable 38
  West's imports of 103
Okudzhava, Bulat 70, 153, 154
Old Continent 33
Oligarchs 57, 58, 62, 63
OPEC+ 141
OPEC, organization of 13
  oil-exporting countries 141
Orbán, Viktor 143
Organization for Economic
  Cooperation and Development
  (OECD) 94, 99

Pacific 20, 65
Pacifism 119
Pact Hitler/Ribbentrop –
  Stalin/Molotov of 1939
  33
Pakistan 20, 77, 91, 108, 114, 128, 147
Palestine 129
Palestinian Islamic Jihad (PIJ) 110
Palestinians 24, 107, 110
Pandemic losses 38, 62, 73, 140
Pandora 149

Panmunjom 44
Papuans 24
Paracel Islands 21
Paraguay 92
Paris 97, 99, 134
Parliamentary obstruction 126
Partnership for Global Infrastructure
  and Investment (PGII) 104
Parys, Jan 33, 34
Patriotic opposition 31
Peace
  fight for 146
  movements 150
  negotiations 40, 41, 67
  settlement 66
  war and 1–3, 149
Peaceful
  coexistence 146
  culture 115
  future 30
  solution 21
Pelosi, Nancy 22, 23, 26, 100, 134
People's Republic of China (PRC) 24, 105
People's anger 49, 51
Peru 92, 105, 127, 141
Peter the Great 84
Petro, Gustavo 127
Petropavlovsk-Kamchatskiy 65
Philippines 20, 88, 91
Phillips curve 79
Phnom Penh 22
Piedmont 76
Pinochet, Augusto 125
Piorun, Polish portable anti-aircraft
  missile set (PPZR) 113
Poland 1, 15, 17, 26, 29–34, 36, 37,
  45, 46, 50, 60, 66, 74, 75, 78,
  79, 83, 91, 93, 94, 96, 97, 99,
  100, 108, 115, 119, 130, 137,
  139, 141
Poles 55, 31
Policy
  anti-China policy of the US 104

anti-inflationary 61
climate 74, 134
economic 76, 77, 79
environmental 151
fiscal 74, 77, 78, 127
monetary 32, 74, 77, 78
of maneuvering between Russia
 and the West 12
progressive 151
social 114
Ukrainian 12
US policy in the Middle East 104
US policy toward Ukraine and
 Russia 36
Polish Academy of Sciences 7
Polish pro-Americanism 33
Political agreement 45
Political deal between Turkey and
 Finland and Sweden 25
Political economy
 of New Pragmatism 2
Political objectives 51, 84
Politics
 a game of influence 101
 and Economics in a Volatile
  World 63, 110
 brutalized in both democracy and
  authoritarianism 130
 great power 14
Polityka 31, 115
Pope Francis 42, 119, 120
Population
 global 136
 immigrant 25
 indigenous 24
 living in poverty 93
 post-working age 139
 Russian population in Ukraine 36
 Ukrainian 15
Populism 127, 149, 150
Portovaya 142
Portugal 124
Power
 balance of 33

Chinese 106
global 1, 91, 102
military 8, 56
of reason 8
Western 14, 102, 109, 113, 119
Pragmatism
 left-wing 127
 new 3, 151, 152
Price increase 62, 73, 74, 76
Prime rate 78
Privatization
 thieving 57
Prokofiev, Sergei 147
Propaganda
 aggressive 115
 neoliberal 58
 pro-Kremlin 115
 pro-regime 55
Prussia 32
Public debt 43, 98, 118, 139
Pugacheva, Alla 70
Pumpyansky, Dmitry 63
Purchasing Power Parity (PPP) 50,
 76, 91, 96, 99, 135
Pushkin, Alexander 8, 69
Putin, Vladimir 8, 11, 14, 16, 22,
 23, 35, 37, 40, 41, 49, 58,
 66–68, 81, 84, 107, 109, 110,
 145, 146
PzH 2000, German howitzer 113

Qatar 114, 141
Queen Elizabeth II 42

Rachmaninoff, Sergei 69
Raisi, Ebrahim 107
Rationality 19
Real estate industry 78
Real income dynamics 78
Realpolitik 45

Recession 61, 76, 80, 93, 149
Refinitiv Datastream 88
Regime
    authoritarian 68, 123, 125, 129, 130
    nostalgia for authoritarian regime 123
    Putin's 58, 65–69
    Russian 81
    Xi Jingping's, authoritarian 68
    Zimbabwe, kleptocratic 50
Regional Comprehensive Economic Partnership (RCEP) 88
Regionalization 89
Re-institutionalization 150
Renault 52
Renewable energy
    implementation program 143
Reparation demands, from Germany 31
Repin, Ilya 8
Resetting the world (dis)order 102
Restrictions
    aimed at reducing the number of citizens participating in elections 126
    anti-Russian 61, 76, 91, 103, 129
    of freedoms and democracy 130
    on the sale abroad of energy carriers 60
Rhodium Group 134
RIA Novosti 115
Riga 100
Romania 27, 36, 124
Rosbalt.ru 115
Round Table 6
Royal castle in Warsaw 52
Royal United Services Institute (RUSI) 59
Russia 1, 2, 6, 7, 11–14, 16, 19, 22, 24–27, 32–46, 49, 50, 52, 56–58, 60–63, 66, 67, 69, 81, 82, 90, 91, 96, 102–104, 106–110, 113, 114, 115, 116, 118, 140–142, 145, 146
Russia's invasion of Ukraine 11, 15, 22, 31, 82, 93, 146
Russian Academy of Sciences 7
Russian army 59
Russian-German condominium 33
Russian language 15
Russian Mir 35
Russians 3, 5, 7, 8, 12, 14, 15, 19, 23, 35, 36, 38–43, 49, 55, 56, 57–59, 65, 67, 69, 70, 74, 81, 82, 84, 90, 91, 98, 104, 109, 115, 116, 129, 141, 146, 147, 149
Russia Today 39, 55
Russophobia 31, 110
Ruto, William 127
Rwanda 52
Rystad 142

SafeGraph 65
Sahrawi 24
Saied, Kais 129
Saigon 147
Sakhalin 8
Sanctions
    commercial, anti-China 51
    committee 52
    economic 50, 55, 56, 59, 67, 90, 91
    effective 49, 52, 59
    foreign 44, 50, 56
    Global Sanctions Database (GSDB) 51
    on Russia 49
    perverse effect (of sanctions) 56, 67
    tariff and non-tariff 89
Sardinians 25
Saudi Arabia 107, 113, 114, 141
Scholz, Olaf 45

Science and Security Board of the
    Bulletin of the Atomic
    Scientists 22
Secretary General of Amnesty
    International 38, 39
Secretary General of United Nations
    41
Security ring around Russia 36
Sejm (lower chamber of the Polish
    parliament) 117
Senate (higher chamber of the Polish
    parliament) 117
Senegal 92, 96
Serbia 124
Seruiratu, Inia 140
Seven plagues of the Bible 149
Severodonetsk 71
Seychelles 92
Sharm el-Sheikh 124
Shining Path 105
Shmyhal, Denys 94, 96
Shock disorders 6
Shortage 37, 51, 62, 73, 76, 79, 80,
    95, 97, 109, 138, 149,
Shortageflation
    3.0 79
    4.0 79
Shostakovich, Dmitry 8, 147
Sibelius, Jean 147
Sieci 34, 115
Sierra Leone 52, 92
Silesia, Lower 15
Siluanov, Anton 57
Simmons, Melinda 16
Singapore 56, 88, 91, 108, 140
Sinophobia 19
Sino-skepticism 105
Slovakia 27, 36, 60
Slumpflation 76
Slump-shortageflation 80
Snyder, Timothy 37, 46
Sochi 65
Social engineering techniques to
    intimidate people 114

Society for Worldwide Interbank
    Financial Telecommunication
    (SWIFT) 57
Solidarity tax 97
Somalia 52, 75
Somaliland 24
Sonora 14
South Africa (Republic of South
    African) 50, 52, 56, 77, 89,
    91, 92, 106, 147
Southern African Development
    Community (SADC) 89, 92
Southern Rhodesia 52, 105
South Korea 88, 89, 108, 114
South Ossetia 102
South Sudan 52
Soviet Union 11, 12, 30, 35, 46,
    102, 115, 147
Spain 15, 27, 68, 77, 114, 119, 123,
    124
Special military operation 8, 40, 42,
    49, 109, 149
Spratly Islands 20
Sputnik 55
Sri Lanka 61, 106
Stagflation 76, 77
Stag-shortageflation 80
Stalingrad 41
Standard of living of the population
    138
Starbucks 65, 67
State capitalism 98
Stoltenberg, Jens 13, 39, 106, 118
St. Petersburg 8, 60, 65, 116
Strait of Hormuz
    blockade 21
Sudan 50, 52, 129
Sustainable development
    economically 152
    environmentally and spatially 152
    socially 152
    strategy of 32
Sweden 55, 84, 106
Swiss Re Institute 134–136

172 Index

Switzerland 15, 25, 56, 59, 97
Syria 24, 83, 110

Taipei 21–23, 27, 100
Taiwan 19–24, 26, 57, 100, 113, 118, 134
Taiwanese 23, 24, 100
Taiwanese Public Opinion Foundation, TFOP 24, 27
Taiwan Strait 24
Tajikistan 20
Taliban 52
Tamaulipas 14
Tanzania 56, 92, 105
Tarapacá 20
Tariffs
  on the import of Chinese products 88
  on US products 88
TASS 115
Tchaikovsky, Pyotr 69
Tebboune, Abdelmadjid 15
Tehran 51, 107
Tel Aviv 110
Telegram 36
Terms of trade 76
Terror
  psychological 8
Texas 126
Thailand 78, 88, 91
Third Rome 35
Thunberg, Greta 146
Tigray 83
Tijuana 14
Togo 45, 92
Trade
  barriers 87
  deficit 89
  war 88, 89
Transnistria 102
Trans-Pacific Partnership (TPP) 87, 88, 92

Transparency International 96
Trudeau, Justin 106
Trump, Donald 46, 87, 128
Truss, Liz 13, 36
Tsinghua University 145
Tunisia 106, 129
Turkey 20, 24, 56, 89, 107, 108, 113, 128
TVN 115
TVP 115
Twitter 56

UFO 6
Uganda 128
Ukraine
  accession of Ukraine to NATO 12
  post-war reconstruction 58, 94, 97
Ukraine's debt 98, 99
Ukrainian catastrophe 7
Ukrainian food exports 37
Ukrainians 5–7, 12–15, 38–42, 56, 63, 66, 67, 70, 82–84, 93, 94, 96, 97, 99–101
UNDP Human Development Index 149
Unemployment 51, 76–80, 93
UN General Assembly 107
UNITA 128
United Arab Emirates 56
United Kingdom 25, 52, 60, 61, 103, 124
United Nations Development Program (UNDP) 93, 99, 149
United Nations High Commissioner for Refugees 82
United States 1, 13, 14, 23, 52, 61, 91, 98, 103, 119, 126, 141, 143, 147, 150
University of Chicago 12
UN Security Council 27, 52, 56
Upper Volta 147

Urban, Jerzy 51
Uruguay 92
USA 50, 56, 59, 69, 78, 99, 106, 134
U.S. Congress 133
U.S. Congress 23, 126
USD 13, 21, 26, 29, 43, 44, 56, 57, 62, 63, 75, 76, 91, 93–96, 98, 104, 108, 120, 133, 134, 135, 136, 140, 141
U.S. House of Representatives 22, 23, 126
USSR 21, 70, 96, 102, 104, 120

Vatican City 27
Venezuela 15, 50, 51, 92, 130, 116
Verdi, Giuseppe 69
Verkhovna Rada Ukrayiny (Verkhovna Rada of Ukraine) 71
Vietnam 1, 15, 20, 56, 66, 88, 91, 105, 147
Vilnius 100
Vkusno i tochka 67
Vladivostok 65
Volgograd 41

War
  Balkan 50
  cold 3, 6, 21, 23, 82, 87, 97, 102–104, 106, 108, 113, 115, 139, 142, 146, 150, 151
  crimes 38, 84
  criminal 49
  First Cold 55, 103, 105, 115, 150
  First World 103
  Hundred-Years' 42
  in Ukraine 8, 39, 42, 61, 62, 66, 73, 74, 89, 107, 108, 115, 129, 142, 145, 149, 152
  of the Pacific, Guerra del Pacífico 20
  Second Cold 101, 103, 107, 108, 144, 150
  Second World 29, 31, 33, 46, 50, 79, 103, 145, 150
  Thirty Years' 42
  Vietnam 1, 66, 105, 147
Warsaw 32, 89
Warsaw Uprising 37
Washington 12, 23, 33, 39, 57, 58, 87
Washington political establishment 58
West 1, 13, 14, 21, 35–37, 44, 49, 51, 55–58, 60, 65–69, 81, 82, 91, 98, 102–109, 115, 145, 147
West Bank 24, 107
West-East 103
Western Sahara 20, 24, 25
White House 22, 52, 58, 88, 104, 125, 133
Winter Olympic Games 145
World Bank 76, 90, 93, 98, 108, 135, 140
World Economic Forum in Davos 66
World Health Organization (WHO) 83
World Population Day 136
World War II 40

Xenophobia 25
Xi Jinping 68, 98, 106

Yankees 15
Yanukovych, Viktor 12
Yeltsin, Boris 62, 104
Yemen 52, 83, 107, 113

Yenisei 60
Yuan 56, 57
Yugoslavia 50, 52
Yushchenko, Viktor 12

Zaldostanov, Aleksandr 45
Zambia 92, 96
ZANU 105
Zelensky, Volodymyr 45, 98
Zimbabwe 50, 52, 92, 105

GPSR Compliance

The European Union's (EU) General Product Safety Regulation (GPSR) is a set of rules that requires consumer products to be safe and our obligations to ensure this.

If you have any concerns about our products, you can contact us on

ProductSafety@springernature.com

In case Publisher is established outside the EU, the EU authorized representative is:

Springer Nature Customer Service Center GmbH
Europaplatz 3
69115 Heidelberg, Germany

www.ingramcontent.com/pod-product-compliance
Lightning Source LLC
LaVergne TN
LVHW011001250326
834688LV00003B/55